On the Communicative Turn in Philosophy

On the Communicative Turn in Philosophy

Exploring Intersubjectivity, Community and the Ethics of Dialogue

Claude Mangion

intellect
Bristol, UK / Chicago, USA

First published in the UK in 2025 by
Intellect, The Mill, Parnall Road, Fishponds, Bristol, BS16 3JG, UK

First published in the USA in 2025 by
Intellect, The University of Chicago Press, 1427 E. 60th Street,
Chicago, IL 60637, USA

A catalogue record for this book is available from the British Library.

Copy editor: MPS Limited
Cover designer: Tanya Montefusco
Indexer: Janet Andrew
Production manager: Tian Greaves
Typesetter: MPS Limited

Hardback ISBN 978-1-83595-163-7
Paperback ISBN 978-1-83595-164-4
ePDF ISBN 978-1-83595-166-8
ePUB ISBN 978-1-83595-165-1

To find out about all our publications, please visit our website.
There you can subscribe to our e-newsletter, browse or download our current catalogue and buy any titles that are in print.

www.intellectbooks.com

This is a peer-reviewed publication.

This text is dedicated to the memory of my parents, Anthony and Amelia Mangion, and my mother-in-law, Utta Klotz.

... soon we shall die and all memory of those five [victims] will have left the earth, and we ourselves shall be loved for a while and forgotten. But the love will have been enough; all those impulses of love return to the love that made them. Even memory is not necessary for love. There is a land of the living and a land of the dead, and the bridge is love, the only survival, the only meaning.

— Thornton Wilder, *The Bridge of Luis Rey*

Contents

Acknowledgements

I want to thank the Rector, Professor Alfred Vella, and the Staff Affairs Committee at the University of Malta for granting me a year's sabbatical leave that enabled me to start my reading and writing. That the University of Malta makes it possible for its academics to take sabbaticals to conduct research demonstrates its commitment to research and the production of knowledge.

On a more personal note, I also want to thank my family – Alain and Caroline – as well as my friends and colleagues for their support during these years. However, most of all, I am grateful to Swantje, for she has had to put up with me the most, sacrificing time and companionship so that I can finish this project.

Introduction

The phrase 'communicative turn' was used by Calvin Schrag in a lecture called 'The communicative turn in the dynamics of philosophical discourse' (2010) to indicate that there was a growing interest in questions related to the interface between the concept of communication and philosophy. A 'turn' means a change of direction or emphasis where a different set of questions takes centre stage; these questions become what Jakobson (1971) calls the 'dominant'. However, the change of dominant does not mean that all other philosophical questions are abandoned but that they take on a secondary role. There have been a number of 'turns' in the history of philosophy: the dominant in the classical period was metaphysical, and the 'turn' that replaced it in the modern period was epistemological. The twentieth century has seen its fair share of 'turns': the postmodern turn, the religious turn, and perhaps the more well-known linguistic turn that, as has been pointed out (Stalmaszczyk and Oleksy 2014), generated a series of turns within it.

Although mainstream philosophers do not, as yet, consider the philosophy of communication as a branch in its own right, instead subsuming it within the philosophy of language as pragmatics, the concept of communication is broader than that of language. Aside from Schrag, several theorists have examined the concept of communication and its intersection with a number of philosophical themes. These include Briankle Chang (1996), Richard Lanigan (1998), John Durham Peters (2001), Garnet Butchart (2019), Bert Olivier (2009) and Ronald Arnett (1986), among others.

This book aims to develop the relationship between communication and philosophy further. In Section A, the guiding question here concerns the issue of intersubjectivity and the purpose is to show that communication always presupposes Others. This can be seen in the work of Husserl, Merleau-Ponty, Schultz and Habermas. In Section B, I examine the relationship between communication and community. The question here concerns how communication can contribute to the formation of a communal identity. To answer this question, I will examine the writings of Carey, Mead, Nancy and Agamben. While it is evident that communication plays a constitutive role in forming a community, the kind of community it can constitute differs radically: for some, it brings people together; for others, it is an opening towards a different kind of community. Section C examines the relationship between communication and the ethics of dialogue. The question guiding this chapter concerns the kind of relations to the Other that dialogical communication entails and in answer to this question, I focus on the writings of Gadamer, Levinas and Bakhtin. What these authors show is that in the dialogical encounter between self and the Other, a certain ethical disposition towards the Other is always presupposed.

What I hope to show by examining these authors in relation to communication is that (a) communication presupposes relations between subjects, (b) who live together in a community and (c) whose dialogical interaction presupposes ethical considerations. I should point out that while the authors taken into consideration have been placed 'neatly' within the respective sections, this segregation has only been followed for analytic purposes. Husserl, for instance, could also have been added to the section on community, and Habermas to the section on the ethics of dialogue. This is true, but it would have gone beyond both the scope of this text as well as the organization of the material and themes.

As with the writing of any book, there are many other authors whom I could have – and perhaps should have – included. While this is true of probably most books, it is also the case that there reaches a point where one has to limit one's reading. I can only justify my decisions by saying that the authors included were the ones that interested me most when it came to researching these themes.

It seems to me that at an institutional level, it is not common to find programmes of study that include the 'philosophy of communication'. Despite this lack of formalization, there is ample research conducted by both philosophers and communication theorists on the intersection between philosophy and communication. This text will hopefully encourage others to conduct further research by aligning communication with questions that are of a philosophical nature.

SECTION A

COMMUNICATION AND INTERSUBJECTIVITY

The question of the existence of Other minds has been one of the indirect questions bequeathed by modern philosophy. Given the radical break between the world of the subject and the world of the object, and given that while the subject can know itself directly and immediately, it could not know whether the Other also has a mind. This has led to the celebrated debate on 'the problem of other minds' where some, such as Ayer (1953), introduced the argument from analogy to justify the existence of Others. On the other hand, Heidegger (1962) has been dismissive of the whole debate because it fails to realize that persons are always primarily situated in a world with Others, so 'the problem of other minds' is a pseudo-problem.

1

Husserl on the Analogous Other

Introduction

The key to Husserl's phenomenology is the intentionality of consciousness. It is key, on his account, because it connects the world of the subject to that of the object, bypassing the lingering and seemingly intractable problems of realism and idealism. What is radically innovative about Husserl's thesis on the intentionality of consciousness is that the subject is no longer opposed to the object but always already correlated with it, such that the dichotomy between them is overcome. To perform this correlation, Husserl introduced the method of bracketing to exclude any presuppositions about the existence of the external world (as the natural sciences presuppose) and the method of reduction to narrow the focus on consciousness. Following these phenomenological procedures makes it possible to analyse anything that appears to consciousness and exclude the unnecessary in the search for the essential meaning. The question of what consciousness and intentionality are about does not discriminate as to whether these are actual physical objects (televisions, trees or cars) or mental states (memory, imagination). It would seem that the concept of communication is marginal to the overall project of Husserl's phenomenology, and some authors (Stawarska 2009) have minimalized its role in his writings. However, as an increasing number of scholars show, this seems to be an overhasty conclusion, and the role of communication in the resolution of the question of intersubjectivity is evident.

In this chapter, I will utilize a number of Husserlian concepts so as to provide a reconstruction of the intentionality of communicative acts against the background of Husserl's theory of intersubjectivity. I will start by first explaining Husserl's theory of signs, with its distinction between indicative and expressive signs, and follow this with his account of intersubjectivity discussed in the *Cartesian Meditations*. In the final section, I will explore the research of Meindl and Zahavi in their elaboration of Husserl's theory of communicative acts. It will become increasingly evident that not only does Husserl tackle the question of solipsism by deploying phenomenological methods to overcome it, but that intersubjective communication is the key to establishing the existence of the objective world.

The nature of signs

By adopting the phenomenological method, Husserl claims that meaning can be constituted objectively, and in the *Logical Investigations*, he identifies logic as 'the science of meaning as such, of their essential sorts and differences' (1970a: 323). It is the discovery of 'essential meanings' that justifies his calling phenomenology a science. But what is crucial for Husserl is the distinction between the invariant or unchanging meaning and the meaning manifested in everyday occurrences (1970a: 229–31). As phenomena appear to consciousness, the subject, by using the method of reduction, uncovers their meaning as intended by consciousness. Intentionality is defined as 'nothing else than this universal fundamental property of consciousness: to be consciousness *of* something; as a *cogito*, to bear within itself its *cogitatum*' (1999: 33, original emphasis). It is the subject that constitutes the 'ideal meanings' that are not relative but the same for everyone. In this sense, they are objective and communicable through language. However, because there is no essential connection between the 'ideality of meanings' and communicative acts, Husserl marginalized the externalization of meaning as it was performed communicatively in his early work.

Husserl undertakes an analysis of signs, differentiating between indicative and expressive signs, proposing a theory of signs that is broad enough to include both objects and language. In the 'Essential distinctions', Husserl seeks to clarify the difference between both signs and starts by pointing to an 'ambiguity' in the term sign; the ambiguity lies in that while indicative signs are not meaningful, expressive signs are, and yet the same word – signs – is applied to both (1970a: 183).

> Indicative signs are non-verbal, indicating or pointing to something: they can be (a) functioning as a 'mark' that enables recognition: 'the brand is a sign of a slave, a flag the sign of a nation'); (b) functioning as 'clues': 'the Martian canals are signs of the existence of intelligent beings on Mars'; and (c) functioning as memory-aids: 'such s the much-used knot in a handkerchief, memorials' (1970a: 183–4184) Indicative signs present themselves and are recognised by the mind: they happen and, in so doing, signify something by pointing to something else through their happening. There is an interesting interplay between the presence of the sign and the absence it points to; indicative signs make present things that are absent. The relation between presence and absence is established on the basis of an association between the sign and what it refers to; we associate one with the other and take this association for granted. Husserl describes the associative relation in terms of 'motivation' because when we see the sign, we are motivated to think about the referent: '*as motivating a belief or surmise in the reality of the other*' [...] In the relation between the two, there is a felt connection in which one points to the other and seems to belong to it.
>
> (1970a: 184, 187, original emphasis)

However, this can be problematic, for it suggests that there is a necessary causal relation between the two, and this is precisely what he wants to exclude from the analysis of indicative signs on the ground that causal explanations belong to the domain of the natural sciences, a domain that is bracketed out as a matter of methodological principle. The signs that Husserl is interested in are those where the association between the indicative sign and what it signifies is conventional or arbitrary in the way that there is nothing intrinsic to a particular flag representing a particular nation.

Expressive signs are linguistic signs combining a material basis in sound or script, involving words and sentences and expressing a meaning:

> If we seek a foothold in pure description, the concrete phenomenon of the sense-informed expression breaks up, on the one hand, in the *physical phenomenon*, forming the physical side of the expression and on the other hand, into the *acts* which give it a *meaning*
>
> (1970a: 191–92, original emphasis)

Expressive signs are meaningful because there is someone who intends a meaning, someone who signifies something through them; otherwise, they would only be noise or scribbles. With expressions – unlike indications – there is a level of meaning that communicates something about a possible state of affairs. It is the mind or consciousness that intends the meaning of communicative acts. Central to the Husserlian account is the speaker whose intentions 'animate' the expression by giving it a meaning. But while Husserl focuses on the speaker's intention to mean, he does not include this criterion with non-verbal gestures such as 'facial expressions'. Although there is a tendency to think that non-verbal gestures are communicative, he excludes them from the class of expressive signs on the grounds that they have no communicative intent because 'one man communicates nothing to another: their utterance involves no intent to put certain "thoughts" on record expressively, whether for the man himself, in his solitary state, or for others. Such "expressions", in short, have properly speaking, *no meaning*' (1970a: 188, original emphasis).

One key feature of expressive signs is that one can understand the meaning of an expression without the object or state of affairs being experienced. There is no need to actually see a sunbed and a beach to understand the expression 'there is a sunbed at the beach'. The meaning of the expression is not connected to the present experience of the object or state of affairs but can also refer to what is absent. The meaning, as ideal, is located in the speaker's intention to mean, locatable in their mind. This leads to the distinction between meaning-conferring acts and meaning-fulfilling acts. In the case of the former, 'meaning-intentions [are] void of intuition' while with the latter, they 'are intuitively fulfilled' (1970a: 192). For both meaning-conferring and meaning-fulfilling acts, the speaker intends to mean something that can be understood, but the difference between them is that with meaning-fulfilling acts, there is a direct relationship to the world. An expressive sign is fulfilled if the object or state of affairs that is being spoken about is present. On the other hand, if the object or state of affairs that is being spoken about is absent, then the intentional meaning is unfulfilled or empty. In other words, meaning-conferring is the attribution of a meaning to an act, while with meaning-fulfilment the act is verified by experience. The crucial point for Husserl is that the former is primary and essential to the meaning of expressive signs, while the latter stands in a logically secondary and nonessential relationship; meaning-conferring acts are 'essential to expression if it is to be an expression at all' (1970a: 192).

When expressive signs are fulfilled, an interesting feature occurs in the way that words seem to fit so closely to the objects that they refer to such that 'the expression seems to be *applied* to the thing and to clothe it like a garment' (1970b: 202, original emphasis). To explain such a close 'fit', Husserl argues that words and objects are connected with a third element, namely the signitive act. Because 'a verbal sign [is] infused with sense' (1970a: 192) words and objects coalesce to form an 'intentional unity' (1970a: 196) such that with the word, we go immediately to the object.

In the sixth *Investigation*, Husserl discusses the theme of categoriality or syntax to explain how individual linguistic signs can be combined into larger units or sentences to communicate. Unlike animal sounds or indicative signs, the combination of human signs generates new meanings that can be communicated to others. Husserl distinguishes between three levels of categoriality: (a) the grammatical aspect of everyday language, (b) the logical grammar of prepositions and (c) the grammar of language through which states of affairs are presented. The third level is especially important because, in the perception of the world, there are certain relations that are not actually seen but that language presents. Husserl again provides an excellent example:

> I can paint *A* and I can paint *B*, and I can paint them both on the same canvas: I cannot, however, paint the *both* nor paint the A *and* the B. Here we have only one possibility which is always open to us: to perform a new act of conjunction or collection on the basis of our two new single acts of intuition, and so *mean* the *aggregate* of the objects *A* and *B*.
>
> (1970b: 291, original emphasis)

Husserl's point is that the logical connectors of the sentence, such as 'both' and 'and', highlight a state of affairs that is more than what is perceived. What this shows is that the use of grammar in the production of sentences is the work of the intellect that goes beyond 'merely sensory perception' by bringing together objects that are on their own in the world.

The analysis of indicative and expressive signs has brought out what they have in common and also what differentiates them in a fundamental manner. Their common feature highlights the role of consciousness as it is directed or intended toward objects in the case of indicative signs and towards words or sentences in the case of expressive signs. The concept of intentionality is the correlation or 'bridge' between the mind or consciousness and things or words and sentences. The analysis of signs shows that it is the mind that can discriminate between indicative and expressive signs.

But while both indicative and expressive signs are intended, there is a fundamental difference between them in that, as Sokolowski explains, indicative signs 'do not possess a meaning that can be quoted, paraphrased, or communicated to someone else by the use of other signs' (2002: 177). For Husserl, while expressive signs signify and express a meaning, indicative signs signify without a meaning; the former 'mean', and the latter 'stand for'. This difference can be brought with Husserl's example of an arabesque: imagine facing an arabesque that you perceive as a decorative sign, as a beautiful form but which, after some time, one realizes is a linguistic sign, perhaps the name of someone. For Husserl, what happens in this shift is that '[t]he whole mode of consciousness changes [...] you see the sign, but you are not focussing on it, you are not intuiting it' (cited in Frechette 2016: 139). The arabesque is no longer a perceptual sign but an expressive one. There is now a shift from the intentionality that perceives the sign to the intentionality that understands the sign as expressive.

The role of linguistic communication is, in early Husserlian phenomenology, clearly considered an obstacle to the search for the 'ideal meaning'. While for Husserl, expression as speech is in a privileged position given the proximity between what is in the speaker's mind and the utterances produced, the problem with it is that if speech involves hearers, i.e. is communicative, then speech also functions indicatively given that the hearer has no immediate access to the mind of the speaker, to what the speaker means. 'If someone utters the wish "I should like a glass of water", this serves to indicate to the hearer the speaker's wish which is also the object of the statement' (1970a: 216). Communicative acts enable mutual understanding to occur because utterances indicate or point to what is in the mind of the Other, to what each intended to mean with their expressions. But for Husserl, the combination of indication with expression 'taints' the purity of the expression, which is why he excludes them from meaningfulness: 'one sees that all expression in communicative speech function as indications' (1970a: 189). The purity of meaning is regained in the sphere of the speaker's 'solitary mental life' (1970a: 190). What this entails is that the speaker has access to the meaning within their mind, and since the meaning is immediate and directly available to speakers there is no need for words or signs as it is pre-linguistic:

> One of course speaks, in a certain sense, even in soliloquy, and it is certainly possible to think of oneself as speaking, and even as speaking to oneself. But in the genuine sense of communication, there is no speech, nor does one tell oneself anything: one merely conceives of oneself as speaking and communicating. In a monologue words can perform no function of indicating the existence of mental acts, since such indication would there be quite purposeless.
>
> (1970a: 191)

On Husserl's account, the physical embodiment of the utterance is unnecessary since it does not contribute to its meaning; they are just media used to transmit the meaning that is located in the intending mind of the speaker. The focus on 'ideal meanings' that are discovered in the mind of the subject leaves the question of the existence of the Other untackled. While the subject knows their own mind, how can they know that the Other has a mind like theirs?

The questions constitute the well-known problem of other minds, the problems that arise out of what Keller calls 'methodological solipsism' (1999: 111–31). As he rightly highlights, Heidegger challenged Husserl's account for a number of reasons. While both agree on the concept of intentionality in their analysis of human existence as providing meaning or sense to human experiences, he challenges Husserl on the grounds that

(a) His account of the intentionality of meaning is essentialist in that it creates a kind of Platonic world where meaning is beyond or outside space and time.
(b) While he introduces the concept of the horizon of meaning within which intentionality is directed and makes sense of experience, this horizon of meaning is internalized by the subject so that, in principle, it can be dislocated from both other persons and the world. For Heidegger, this account places too much emphasis on meanings as mental states that are presented to the self for examination.
(c) His account preserves the traditional opposition of essence and existence, of the actual and the potential, with the concept of intentionality as constituting a 'fixed' essence or nature of humans, in the same way as objects or animals have a nature.

The introduction of Dasein to describe human existence by Heidegger counters Husserlian phenomenology of the solitary self. Dasein has no fixed human nature characterized by a set of properties. From the framework of the actual-potential distinction, Dasein is the being whose existence is marked by its possibilities, while the existence of objects or animals is marked by the actualization of their properties. So, too, Heidegger rejects the whole notion of internal mental states that are available and understood by the subject, arguing instead that mental states can only be understood by Dasein's practical engagement with the world. When Heidegger writes that Dasein exists as a being-in-the-world, he is positioning himself against the dominant Cartesian model that opposes the subject to the object – whether other persons or objects (natural or man-made). As opposed to this dichotomy, the existence of Dasein is relational, always already embedded in a world that includes others and objects and, therefore, a world that is spatially constituted.

Given that Husserl's 'methodological solipsism' isolates the subject in a self-contained world of meanings, can communication provide a way out of this world?

Communication

In the Introduction to the *Logical Investigations,* Moran writes, 'Communication is not Husserl's concern because, for him, logic is concerned only with the *expression* of ideal meanings. The pragmatics of communication or reception of meaning is a secondary matter, a concern for the philosopher of language' (1970a: L, original emphasis). This is a frequent criticism of Husserl. Sokolowski points out that Husserl's model of communication neglects the role of the hearer in the communicative act, with the hearer as 'merely' the flip side of the speaker. Husserl does not explain the actual connection that communication brings about between the mind of the speaker and the mind of the hearer: 'words link the speaker and listener in one common train of thought [...] [t]he receptivity of the listener should be added to the dimensions of speech' (Sokolowski 2002: 182–23). So too Butchart argues that by thinking of meaning as constituted within the mind of the subject the hearer is neglected in Husserl's account of communication: 'If meaning is understood by the transcendental phenomenologist to originate in the relation of consciousness *to itself* ... then the question of social interaction emerges, and specifically the formation of meaning within interaction' (Butchart 2017: 60, original emphasis).

However, these views have been indirectly challenged by Meindl and Zahavi (2023), who, in a recent paper entitled 'From communication to communalisation: A Husserlian account', make a strong case to argue that, contrary to the views mentioned above, Husserl recognized the centrality of communication and its trajectory to the formation of community. They take as their point of departure Stawarska's claim that 'classical phenomenology [...] privileges first-person subjectivity over against communal relationality and leads to the neglect of I-you connectedness' (2009: ix–x) because its point of departure is the detached I, who is unable to 'break' out of their ego to communicate with the other. On this account, Husserl most notably failed to recognize the contribution of the Other in forming a society that he theorized as an aggregation of individuals.

Meindl and Zahavi disagree with her assessment of Husserl and argue that, on the contrary, Husserl was very concerned with the nature and role of communication (2023: 2). While the concept of communication rarely features in *Cartesian Meditations*, they identify three areas where the concept of communication plays a fundamental role in Husserl's phenomenology of interest with communication: (a) the first concerns the establishment of the objectivity of the external world through intersubjective agreement, an agreement that is constituted through communicative interaction; (b) the second concerns the formation of the self, where the sense of a self is produced through its interaction with others and (c) the third concerns Husserl's insistence on the role of communication in the constitution of society.

As with Husserl's phenomenology, Meindl and Zahavi point out that intentionality is the key feature of his concept of communication. For communicative interaction to occur, the listener must recognize that the speaker intends to communicate with them. Only in this way is a connection between them established, for it is quite possible to use language or act in a way that might not affect the Other. Unless the Other recognizes the intention to communicate, for Husserl, this cannot be considered a communicative act: '[it] belongs to the normal concept of communication that while I am [...] carrying out the communication (*Mitteilung*), I am at the same time understood (experienced) by the Other as an I acting in this way' (cited in Meindl and Zahavi 2023: 365). But there is a further element that needs to be taken into any account of communicative interaction, for it is not only the recognition of the communicative intention by the listener that provides the basis for the constitution of an I-You relation. What is also required is that the listener acknowledges the speaker's communicative intentions. Husserl, as Meindl and Zahavi show, adopts and elaborates upon the idea of 'uptake' that he appropriated from Reinach (2012). The critical difference between their views on the acknowledgement of the intention is that the latter focused narrowly on legal discourses in contrast to Husserl, who was interested in everyday communicative interaction:

> The communication as such is accepted (ubernommen), is registered (aufgenommen). My wish to communicate [...] reaches into the appresented other, by virtue of the other carrying out the activity of appropriation, of engaged listening (engehendes Zuhoren) – which evinces itself for me in the understanding of the other as a listener, evinces itself on the basis of the outward posturing of the other which 'expresses' [the act of] listening in the first sense.
>
> (cited in Meindl and Zahavi: 367)

Husserl's account firmly places the role and response of the addressee as crucial to the dynamic of communication: for communicative interaction to take place, the addressee must express to the speaker their response to the original communicative act. When this occurs, there is a mutual interlocking of intentions between speaker and listener, constituting the basis of everyday communication. And while mutual understanding is the ground for agreement or disagreement, it does not necessarily imply that they agree with what each other says. The point is that continuing communication would not be possible without this preliminary understanding of each other's intentions.

Interestingly, as Meindl and Zahavi point out, Husserl's theory of communication does not belong to the instrumentalist view of communication, where communication is 'merely' a tool used to persuade or change the listener's mind. Rather, Husserl's theory of communication is holistic in the sense that through their communicative interactions, participants create a we-world where 'the communicative intertwinement is a joint accomplishment of both addresser and addressee and cannot just be established by the former alone' (2023: 8).

Intersubjectivity

While the analysis of signs in the *Logical Investigations* entails an implicit recognition of the Other subject, the question of interpersonal and intentional communication between subjects takes on a more central place in *Ideas II*. Husserl writes: 'It should be noted here that the *idea of communication* obviously extends from the single personal subject *even to the social* associations of subjects, which for their part present personal unities of a higher level' (1990: 206, original emphasis). This claim lies on the basis of Gilicka's argument (2017) that the overall project of phenomenology cannot work if intersubjective communication is not part of the analysis of intersubjectivity relations. It is her contention that while the *Cartesian Mediations* focuses more specifically on the question of intersubjectivity, many of the concepts in this text are introduced in *Ideas II* such that it can contribute to a fuller understanding of the former. For my purposes, I will be focussing chiefly on the *Meditations*, although I will refer to *Ideas I* and *II* to consolidate certain points.

Husserl considered *Ideas* as not having taken 'the proper consideration of transcendental solipsism or transcendental intersubjectivity', and this lack of consideration led him to specify that the *Meditations* 'contain an essential supplement or the detailed treatment of the fundamental problem of transcendental intersubjectivity, wherein the solipsistic objection completely collapses' (cited in Haney 1988: 32). But, the key point for Husserl is that while the problem of solipsism is explicitly stated as in need of resolution, this is part of the larger question concerned with establishing the existence of the external – natural and social – world. Given that Others are part of the analysis of the objective world, I will describe Husserl's analysis of Others, keeping in mind that although Husserl distinguishes between the natural and social/cultural words, both are framed as existing 'there-for-all'. It is increasingly evident, at this stage, why the problem of Other minds is one that Husserl needs to resolve: if phenomenology claims to describe the objective world, and if, in turn, this presupposes Others, then the resolution of the question concerning the existence of Others is an important step in establishing the existence of the objective world. Haney stresses the importance of this: '[t]he rejection of Husserl's doctrine of intersubjectivity is tantamount to a rejection of Husserl's systematic philosophy, and because without it there is no bridge between consciousness and the world' (1988: 33).

Having bracketed out, in the first *Meditation*, the existence of all objects in the world, including the existence of Others (as objects in the world) and in the second *Meditation*, Husserl outlines the problem of Other minds from the perspective of phenomenological methodology: by focussing on the subject as the constituter of meaning, it cannot avoid being solipsistic: phenomenology 'begins accordingly as a pure egology and as a science that apparently condemns us to a solipsism' (1999: 30). This is precisely the problem: if phenomenology takes as its point of departure the subject, then how can it explain the existence of Other subjects: 'But what about other egos, which are not a mere intending and intended *in me*, merely as synthetic unities of possible verification *in me*, but according to their sense, precisely as *others*?' (1999: 89, original emphasis).

The problem is further accentuated because phenomenology does not even require the existence of Others. However, Husserl is convinced that the existence of Others is part of the development of phenomenology (1999: 30–31) and in the fifth *Meditation*, he introduces a second bracketing procedure that excludes the world of intersubjectivity since the existence of Others is implied in the experience of the natural and social/cultural worlds. What is achieved by this exclusion, at least at this stage, is the possibility of the self-focussing on its own consciousness: this is why Husserl calls it the 'sphere of ownness' since it is the sphere of experiences that belongs to a specific self as opposed to experiences that Others also have.

The reduction to the 'sphere of ownness' is undertaken by a process of 'abstraction from everything that transcendental constitution gives me as Other' (1999: 93). However, the terminology of abstraction should not mislead, for it is not used in the customary sense of abstracting from particulars to produce cognitively a general idea. This intellectual process enables one to establish similarities between things or parts with a general idea in common. But for Husserl, the concept of abstraction is spontaneous and serves the double purpose of excluding what is different from the self and constituting the self as a subject with its own world, its own 'sphere of ownness'. The second reduction describes the experiences that only the subject can have; it is a self-enclosed world.

Husserl remarks that the reduction to the sphere of ownness leaves one with an experience that constitutes a 'founding stratum': it is a reduction to a basic level of pure consciousness. This founding stratum is one where '*we retain a coherent stratum of the phenomenon world*' (1999: 96) by which Husserl wants to point out that it is not a fragmented or disjointed state. The 'founding stratum' shows that by starting from the self, one can prove the existence of the Other and, ultimately, the existence of the objective world: 'I obviously cannot have the "alien" or "other" as experience, and therefore cannot have the sense "Objective world" as an experiential sense, without having this stratum in actual experience; whereas the reverse is not the case' (1999: 96).

The value of the second reduction is that it reinstates that which was bracketed out by the first reduction, i.e. the whole domain of sensations, feelings and the body. The analysis of the 'sphere of ownness' reveals that each subject has its own particular 'Nature': it is the experience of each and every subject as opposed to the concept of nature in the customary sense of objective nature that is studied by natural scientists and is the same for all (1999: 96). An essential feature of the self's 'Nature' is that it enables the subject to experience its body as something it feels and controls. Through its body, the subject interacts with the world such that the body is experienced as an 'animate organism' that, in addition, has a mind. The 'sphere of ownness' that results from the second reduction orients the analysis towards what belongs exclusively to the subject, namely the unity of body and mind, a psycho-physical identity constituted in its totality as an 'animate organism'.

> Bringing to light my animate organism, reduced to what is included in my ownness, is itself part of bringing to light the *ownness-essence* of the objective phenomenon: '*I, as this man.*' if I reduce other men to what is included in my oneness, I get bodies included therein; if I reduce *myself* as a man, I get '*my animate organism*' and my '*my psyche*', or myself as a *psychophysical unity.*
>
> (1999: 97, original emphasis)

One important consequence of this formulation is that, unlike Descartes, Husserl frames consciousness as embodied (Haney 2002: 150). Given that the subject is a 'psycho-physical unity', the question that Husserl seeks to answer is: what are the essential features that constitute the subject, features without which it would not be a subject? What are the 'structural forms' that constitute the nature of the subject?

By taking a step back, the subject can examine or perceive its own 'structural forms': a phenomenological self-examination reveals that (a) it perceives itself as existing and continuing to do so in the future, with the term 'perception' being used in a broad sense to include both having memories and intentions and therefore, of having a past and a future; (b) it perceives its 'immanent temporality' by which it endures or retains an identity over time, despite being subject to change and also introducing change; it has a perception of itself that, in turn, constitutes its identity. However, the analysis of the self has so far only established the existence of the self, so the question concerning the existence of the Other remains unanswered.

While the individual self experiences its body in a certain way and while the body of the Other has its own experiences, both bodies are similar to each other by being 'animate organisms'. To highlight the similarity of bodies, Husserl introduces the term 'analogical apperception' with the term 'apperception' fulfilling the double role of perceiving the Other and oneself. Analogical apperception is important because it enables the 'transfer of sense': the experiences of the self are transferred to the experiences of the Other body: to be 'apprehended as an animate organism, [the body] must have derived this sense by an *apperceptive transfer from my own animate organism*' (1999: 110, original emphasis). The 'analogical apperception' of the Other is immediate and not due to logical inference or some particular perception of Others. It is a common everyday experience that arises whenever we see two similar objects: '*each everyday experience* involves an *analogizing transfer* of an originally instituted objective sense to a new case, with its anticipative apprehension of the object as having a similar sense' (1999: 111, original emphasis). There has been much debate on the role and value of analogy within the *Meditations*, with Ricoeur (1967) considering it to be a crucial part of the fifth *Meditation* insofar as it enables Husserl to overcome solipsism.

The role of 'analogical apperception' is fundamental to establishing the existence of the Other through (a) the concept of pairing, and (b) spatial location

(a) The concept of pairing describes a common feature of human experience. It occurs when two similar objects are perceived together and classified as belonging to the same kind. With humans, one is aware of one's body as an 'animate organism' so that when one perceives the body of the Other, one is aware that both bodies constitute a pair of similar things. However, there is a key difference between the pair in that the self has direct experience of its life as it is lived, but not that of the Other. The world that the Other experiences – its sensations, movements, and intentions – is precisely its own world and cannot be experienced by the self. However, Husserl adds that the behaviour of the Other functions as a marker of how one would expect another 'animate organism' to behave. If the Other were not an 'animate organism', its behaviour would expose this: 'the organism becomes experienced as a pseudo-organism, precisely if there is something discordant about its behaviour' (1999: 114).
(b) The spatial location of the Other: both the body of the self and that of the Other are positioned in relation to each other so that while one body is 'here',

> the Other is 'there'. Clearly, they do not each occupy the same physical space, but for human bodies, the possibility of changing location suggests that the self can occupy the space of the Other over 'there' while the Other can occupy the space over 'here'. What this means for Husserl is that through 'locomotion, I can change my position in such a manner that I can convert any There into a Here – that is to say, I could occupy any spatial locus with my organism' (1999: 116). In this respect, it is obvious that they cannot be occupying the same space: if the Other is not occupying the space 'here' because I am occupying it, then the body must belong to someone else to another self.

Husserl introduces the concept of empathy to explain how the self understands the mental states of the Other: 'for example: as the outward conduct of someone who is angry or cheerful, which I easily understand from my own conduct in similar circumstances' (1999: 120). 'Analogical apperception' enables the self to understand the mental states of the Other because it takes its own mental states as the point of departure to interpret the external behaviour of the Other as a sign of their mental states. The role of empathy – as a face-to-face encounter with the Other – has been central to accounts of intersubjectivity. This line of approach is contested by Zahavi, who argues that there are other ways of explaining intersubjectivity without restricting it to face-to-face encounters. These have included intersubjectivity as relationships that are established between embodied subjects or as an account that presupposes the existence of a world that is always already there prior to face-to-face encounters or those accounts that posit the Other as a radical other. Zahavi argues that each of these accounts is lopsided, so an adequate account of intersubjective relations must be systematic and inclusive of these various facets (2001: 166).

The solution to the problem of solipsism takes on, with Husserl, a novel form: while the self is directly present to itself and experiences its own world, the Other is only indirectly present to the self. And in the same way, the Other experiences its world directly and the world of the self indirectly. Husserl overturns the problem of solipsism – as the inability to know the existence of their minds – into its solution because the inability to know the mind of the Other shows that there is a mind – the mind of the Other – that transcends the self.

Given that he establishes the existence of others, Husserl argues that it is the same world within which the self and others inhabit.

> It is implicit in the sense of my successful apperception of others that their world, the world belonging to their appearance-systems, must be experienced forthwith as the same as the world belonging to my appearance-systems; and this involves an identity of our appearance-systems.
>
> (1999: 125)

Because the self and the Other are both 'animate organisms' with the same natural bodies, while they perceive the world from different perspectives, it is the same world that they perceive. By starting from others as existing 'objects' in the world, independently of the subject, Husserl goes on to show that the common nature of both necessarily entails that they experience an objective world: '[t]he existence-sense of the world and of Nature in particular, as Objective Nature, includes after all, as we have already mentioned, thereness-for-everyone. This is always cointended wherever we speak of Objective actuality' (1999: 92). The doctrine of intersubjectivity fulfils the need to establish the existence of the world without presupposing its existence (as with realism) or its being vouchsafed by God.

From this, Husserl goes on to develop a theory of community, of what he calls 'communalization' to argue that a community is not just an agglomeration of isolated subjects but one where subjects are in 'communion' – communicate – with each other. Meindl and Zahavi (2023) point out that the analysis of communication in Husserl is not restricted to relations between subjects but also several subjects as they communicate about something in the world; in this case, one person wants to attract the attention of the other towards something else. The upshot of Husserl's account of them is that by introducing the idea of shared communication as being about something in the world, the world becomes a shared or common world. In other words, the objectivity of the world is presupposed for there to be something to communicate about. Meindl and Zahavi say this eloquently: '[w]ithout being embedded in a common temporal and spatial framework, we would be able to perceive each other, and communication would never get off the ground' (Meindl and Zahavi 2023). This is a crucial point, for it shows that communication presupposes intersubjective relations.

The *Cartesian Mediations* have enabled Husserl to establish two key points: (a) the existence of others and (b) the existence of the objective world. Given that the first reduction has excluded the Other, if communication entails others, then there is no communication at this stage. However, by establishing the existence of others from the position of the self, Husserl shows that others are always there in the world. In effect, communication presupposes intersubjective relations and crucially for Husserl, it is through intersubjective agreement that the existence of the world as the same for all is established.

Conclusion

Husserl had high hopes that the phenomenological method, with its series of reductions and bracketing, would enable philosophy to achieve status on a par with other 'scientific' disciplines. Central to this method was the role of intentionality as the basic structure of consciousness, with the objects of consciousness as intentional objects such that there was a correlation between consciousness and objects. However, it would be misleading to think of Husserl as focussing primarily or exclusively on questions of method, for several of his writings attest to his interest in the application of phenomenology to human life as it unfolded culturally, historically and institutionally.

Husserl's early account of meaning is problematic, for it fails to explain whether other subjects exist apart from the one in whom meanings are discovered. However, in his later writings, he attempts to establish the existence of others without emphasizing the role of communication, and this seems to support the claim that communication played a marginal role in his phenomenological project. Recent research shows that this is not the case and that communication plays a more fundamental role in his writings. In particular, it can be claimed that communication always presupposes intersubjective relations that are transformed into a community.

2

Merleau-Ponty on the Embodied Other

Introduction

Merleau-Ponty's interest in language and communication spanned throughout his writings, with varying shifts of emphasis, but this interest is also reflected in the various ways he articulates the relationship between communication – from perceptual to linguistic – and intersubjectivity. His point of departure is the embodied nature of self, with the corollary being that the Other – as another subject – is also embodied. Embodiment is the basis of prelinguistic intersubjective relations with communication as furthering the interaction between self and Others in producing a 'we' world. By focusing on speech as a lived experience, Merleau-Ponty shifts the analysis of language away from linguistic theories that studied language as an 'object' – objectively – since this excluded the speaking subject from the language itself.

In the first section, I will discuss his rejection of the objectification of language typified by Saussurean linguistics; following this, I will then focus on his analysis of language as a 'lived experience' of subjects and finally show that such an experience is shared by other subjects. What I aim to show is that the question of the relationship between communication and intersubjectivity is cemented with Merleau-Ponty's phenomenological account of speech as a 'lived experience' insofar as this experience has existential dimensions that itself presuppose the existence of Others.

The problem with Saussurean linguistics

In several of his writings, Merleau-Ponty turns his attention to linguistics, particularly the linguistic theories of Saussure. On the latter's account, linguistics should strive to emulate the natural sciences by studying language objectively as a 'science' of language. For, the idea that *langue* should be studied by using the methodologies of the physical sciences so as to discover the meaning was a non-starter: 'There is no analysis of language capable of making language crystal clear and arraying it before us as if it were an object' (2002: 455). As he will argue, if one focuses on the objectivity of language, then what is crucial about it – the speaking subject – would be, paradoxically, abandoned from language.

Saussurean linguistics introduced several innovative and fundamental concepts to the study of language:

(a) it considered the study of linguistics from a historical perspective to be irrelevant to the study of language, for the change of word meanings over time cannot explain the way a language works to generate meanings. Knowing how a word evolved into its current usage makes no difference to a speaker. To support his claim, Saussure introduced the crucial distinction between *langue* and *parole* while highlighting the primacy of *langue* (1983). The two domains had different foci: *langue* was the institutional and sedimented system of rules and meanings that constituted the network of a language, while *parole* was the executive side of language, actualizing the rules and meanings to produce speech. With this distinction, Saussure differentiated between the necessary features of a language as a system from the contingent features of a language as speech. It was because *langue* constituted the system or structure of language that, Saussure felt, his claim to the scientific objectivity of language was justified, as opposed to speech, which involved too many variables (from the intentions, moods as well as the Other whom the speaker is addressing) to qualify as the object of scientific study.
(b) it highlighted the arbitrary nature of the sign where he argues that the relation between the signifier and the signified is arbitrary, i.e. non-necessary. This claim highlights the social and conventional aspects of language and meaning with the spoken word as the speaker's use of the conventional system institutionalized by language. As the emphasis on the conventional and the institutional shows, it should be clear that just because the relation between the signifier and the signified is arbitrary, the speaker is not at liberty to use words to mean whatever they want.
(c) it formulated the principle of difference or differentiation: this is the claim that meaning is the result of the relation between words or signs, as opposed to the idea that the meaning of a word or sign is the thing it names. In other words, the meaning of a word or sign is constituted internally by its difference from other signs. A language is, therefore, a system or network of differences, such that to know the meaning of a word or sign is to understand what it is different from. Words or signs do not exist in isolation but in what Saussure describes as a negative relation to each other.

Merleau-Ponty acknowledges the importance of the principle of differentiation in the generation of meaning for signs 'taken one by one signify nothing;

they succeed in conveying signification only through their assembly, just as communication passes from the whole of spoken language to the whole of understood language' (1973: 42). The principle of differentiation coupled with combination transforms language from a static phenomenon to a dynamic one with the consequence that language is no longer just a tool for communication but an open-ended and incomplete system of possibilities at the discretion of the speaker: 'speaking is not having at one's disposal a certain number of signs. Speaking is possessing language as a principle of distinction' (1973: 32).

In addition, Merleau-Ponty argues that the benefit of Saussure's account is that it dispelled several myths: these are (a) the myth of a pure language which depicts language as a transparent medium, i.e. the representational theory of language, taking or leading us directly to the world; it is a myth that has language 'deliver us from language by delivery us to things' (1973: 4); (b) the myth of a 'universal language' (1973: 7) that identifies a foundational language that could then be used to explain other specific languages. Merleau-Ponty observes that this is what Husserl had in mind in the *Logical Investigations* when he strived to find a 'universal grammar which would establish the forms of signification indispensable to every language' (1964: 84). Paradoxically, this account could only end in failure, for Husserl's attempt to find a 'pure grammar' led to a 'language without words' (1973: 6).

Despite Merleau-Ponty's acknowledgement of Saussure's innovative contributions to the study of language, he shifts the priority of this study away from the emphasis on language as an abstract and timeless system governed by rules to a study that focuses on the subject, on the experience of the speaking subject. What is required, he argued, was 'a return to the speaking subject, to my contact with the language I am speaking' (1964b: 85). By focusing on the speaker's relation to meaning, Merleau-Ponty presents a dynamic view of language, a dynamism that makes possible the change of meanings over time and for creativity to be central to language itself.

The opposition between a static and a dynamic account of meaning explains Merleau-Ponty's distinction between primary and secondary speech. The primary or 'originating speech' is that of the constituted meanings, of the institutional fact of language as a repository of words and meanings; this is the inherited language humans learn to communicate with others. But, if a language were just composed of primary speech, there would be nothing but repetition; language, in effect, would be transformed into a static and unchanging entity: 'it is therefore necessary to conceive the operation of speech as outside any previously institutionalised signification, as a unique act whereby a man's speaking furnishes his listener and a culture that is common to them' (1973: 141).

The origin of meaning

Given Merleau-Ponty's valorization of lived speech, the question that needs to be accounted for concerns the meaning that the self communicates. The self is no longer a disembodied Cartesian mind or consciousness that is dislocated from its embodied being in the world because 'I am my body' (2002: 231). Merleau-Ponty radically rearticulates the concept of the body so that it is no longer considered an object within a world of objects. Instead, his account gives the body a primary position in that it becomes 'the place of a certain view of the world' by virtue of its 'position in relation to the vertical, the horizontal, and certain other axes of important coordinates of its environment' (1964: 117) by being locked into a position the body generates an 'aura' of meaning that is not just a question of anatomical structure. In addition, the meaningfulness of the body endows it with a transcendence that reaches out to other bodies and the world; it is a signifying power transcending its biological makeup. The importance of this account is that it situates the body within the world as signifying intentionality; it is the origin of 'sense' or meaning, and as a result, it will 'reveal to us the perceiving subject as well as the perceived world' (2002: 83). There is explicit parallelism between the relationship between the embodied self and the world and the embodied self and the Other: '[i]t is through my body that I understand other people just as it is through my body that I perceive "things"' (2002: 216). It is therefore the body that constitutes the condition of possibility for understanding others – who also have a body – and the world given that the embodiment of self and Other enables the objectivity of the world to be constituted as the same for all.

This description of the body has significant consequences as it shifts the Cartesian way of thinking about the body as one object within a world of objects to the body as a 'means of communication with [the world]' (2002: 95). Merleau-Ponty re-directs the analysis of meaning away from a strictly linguistic or propositional account to a broader phenomenological one in which the perceptual structures of the body are sources of meaning, with linguistic meaning as a furthering of the perceptual. Within the perceptual field, the situated body is already meaningful by virtue of its interaction within a world of meaning. As Johnson (2006: 3) points out, babies and children experience a world of meaning in their daily lives even before the acquisition of linguistic meaning.

Given Merleau-Ponty's centrality of the body as the matrix of meaning, the question that arises concerns the connection between the body and 'the phenomenon of speech'. This will entail an analysis of the concept of meaning, which will involve an engagement with the dominant empiricist and intellectualist accounts of meaning (2002: 202–35), as both accounts fail to articulate the body's relationship to speech. By drawing out the logical conclusions of these two accounts,

Merleau-Ponty showed the untenability of both as explanatory models since they attempt to explain speech in terms of something else to achieve clarity. With the empiricist account, meanings are verbal images triggered by distinct sounds through a process of stimulus and response such that speech and the production of meaning become entirely mechanical. As Merleau-Ponty points out, this account is unsatisfactory because it examines speech as an 'object', as a kind of thing that is studied from a third-person perspective. Furthermore, and paradoxically, it excludes the speaker from the communicative act: 'there is no speaker, there is a flow of words set in motion independently of any intention to speak' (2002: 203). The intellectualist account of meaning is explained by recourse to a consciousness that projects meaning into words. The problem here is that meaning is located in the cognitive sphere with the result that the word itself does not actually have a meaning; it is more like a container into which meaning is poured. In this case, meaning is a function of thinking rather than a speaking subject. But for Merleau-Ponty, it is precisely because meaning is connected with the speaking subject that he counters intellectualist and empiricist theories with the assertion, 'the word has a meaning' (2002: 206). Theories of linguistic meaning that fail to explain the experience of speech in its existential context serve instead to reinforce self-world dualism.

There is a further question that Merleau-Ponty needs to examine in order to dispel the dualism of thought and linguistic expression with the latter as the communication of the former. An analysis of the relation between thought and expression (2002: 202–35) shows that (a) a thought is not 'enclosed' within a word that represents it, and (b) a thought does not function as a sign of the nervous system. What he proposes instead is that thought and speech are mutually entwined so as to dismantle the traditional opposition between the inner and the outer: 'In trying to describe the phenomenon of speech and the specific act of meaning, we shall have the opportunity to leave behind us, once and for all, the traditional subject-object dichotomy' (2002: 202). This traditional formulation represented by Descartes and Kant, has privileged thought over speech, with speech as an accidental feature useful only for the communication of thought. For Merleau-Ponty, the opposite is the case: he argues that there is a necessary connection between thought and speech and, by way of example, describes the situation of the orator who – in an act of improvisation – does not think first and speak later but rather, his thoughts emerge with his words, 'his speech is his thought' (2002: 209). For the audience, the speech is the presentation of his thoughts, and it is only after the speech has ended that the audience judges the speech: '[t]here is thus, either in the man who listens or reads, or in the one who speaks or writes, a *thought in speech* the existence of which is unsuspected by intellectualism' (2002: 209, original emphasis). In addition, Merleau-Ponty argues that the relationship between thought and speech is dialectical: thought needs speech to be expressed, but speech, in turn, affects thought by organizing it by sharpening what might have been hazy. It is a relationship where each 'puts out a branch into the other' (1964b: 18).

But while thought and speech are mutually connected, they are clearly not identical; perhaps a better way to describe their relationship would be to say that they are 'fused'. This can be seen in the following analogy: for Merleau-Ponty, just as life requires embodiment for its fulfilment, thought requires language for its fulfilment or 'completion'. Language is the incarnation of thought requiring 'the experience of its presence in the flesh of speech' (1964b: 91). This is why there can be no such thing as a thought in itself: 'A thought limited to existence for itself, independently of the constraints of speech and communication, would no sooner appear than it would sink into the unconscious, which means that it would not exist even for itself' (2002: 202).

Given the emphasis on the shared world of significance that both the self and the Other inhabit, it is no surprise that Merleau-Ponty is critical of the linear model of communication. The commonplace view of communication as linear frames communication as the transmission of a message from the speaker to the listener. In this model, the meaning or thought is in the speaker's mind, and they encode it and transmit it to a listener, who decodes the meaning to reach its destination in their mind. This model assumes a dichotomy between the meaning or thought and the language used to communicate that meaning or thought; on this account, the medium is incidental to the communication of the message. Merleau-Ponty challenges this point: 'Our analyses of thought give us the impression that before it finds the words which express it, it is already a sort of ideal text that our sentences attempt to *translate*' (1964: 42–43, original emphasis).

Speech is, therefore, not merely the transmission of a meaning that is located within the speaker's mind but, crucially, a positioning of the subject within a 'world of his meanings' (2002: 225). This is why Merleau-Ponty calls upon us to recognize the 'existential significance in speech' (2002: 225). But there is a further crucial dimension to language: it transforms the world that is inherently significant into a world that is a linguistic system of significance. Quite rightly, Merleau-Ponty considers the linguistic world as a 'universe': 'it [language] in turn becomes something like a universe, and it is capable of lodging things themselves in this universe – after it has transformed them into their meaning' (1964: 43).

Given that the spoken word embodies a meaning, the question that arises is from where does this meaning originate? Merleau-Ponty's analysis of the origin of speech will take him to the body and its gestural expressions: '[t]he spoken word is a genuine gesture, and it contains its meaning in the same way as the gesture contains its. This is what makes communication possible' (2002: 213). The link between speech as gesture and gesture itself is that both communicate or express a 'sense' or meaning: both are modes of intentionality that position the subject within the world. The connection between the self and the Other(s) is reconfirmed with both the spoken expression as a gesture and the gestural expressions of the body:

> The phonetic 'gesture' brings about, both for the speaking subject and for his hearers, a certain structural co-ordination of experience, a certain modulation of existence, exactly as a pattern of my bodily behaviour endows the objects around me with a certain significance both for me and from others.
>
> (2002: 225)

Although a gesture is silent, it is not an emptiness without any sense but rather a silence full of possible senses. Likewise, language is an open and incomplete system that always makes it possible for new senses to be expressed. While the establishment of language marks a rupture from 'the mute communication of gesture' (2002: 225), the connection between them is formed by a trajectory of sense or meaning.

In 'The body as expression and speech' (2002: 202–32), Merleau-Ponty identifies several features of gestural meaning:

(a) it is embodied: the body that expresses the sense of its gestures and is central to both the perception of things) as well as the understanding of linguistic communication).
(b) it is pre-cognitive: when one looks at another person's external behaviour, one does not have to go through a process of deduction to understand that person's mental state. The meaning of external behaviour is its mental state.
(c) it is not a sign of something else, nor are they the cause of something else. There is no 'behind' to the gesture to get to the meaning; the meaning is the gesture and its presentation within a world. When we see an angry person, we do not first try to remember the feelings we had when we used the same angry gestures so as to understand what the gestures mean, and neither do we need to think of the gesture as a sign of something else, as though the sign is merely an external tool for an internal meaning.
(d) it requires a common experiential experience: there is a shared existential basis that enables the meaning of the gesture to be understood. For Merleau-Ponty, a child would be unable to understand a sexual scene until it reached a certain sexual maturity.
(e) it entails an understanding of the intentions of each participant within a communicative interaction; these intentions are expressed through the body.

With the grounding of speech in gesture, Merleau-Ponty dismantles another contemporary dualism that opposes gesture as natural signs to language as conventional signs. Such an opposition is no longer tenable for

> was not the communication of the elements of language between the 'first man to speak' and the second necessarily of an entirely different kind from communication to gesture? This is what is commonly expressed by saying that gesture or emotional pantomime are 'natural signs', and the world a 'natural convention'.
>
> (2002: 217)

His strategy for dismantling this opposition is to show how each term contains elements of its opposite. To begin with, the thesis that language is conventional fails to recognize that it is constructed upon something more fundamental, on a more original form of communication. It is, in fact, 'a late form of relationship between men; they presuppose an earlier means of communication, and language must be put back into the current of intercourse' (2002: 217). The 'earlier means of communication' refers precisely to an originary gestural meaning. With the opposite thesis that gestures are natural, Merleau-Ponty claims that this view has been challenged by anthropologists and social psychologists who point out that what might be considered a natural emotion in one culture varies in others. In other words, even gestures can be read according to the cultural context of their production.

Johnson (2006: 6–7) calls Merleau-Ponty's account 'The embodied theory of meaning' with its key characteristics being: (a) the interaction between persons and their environment; (b) the relation between a part and the whole: '[i]t is about how one thing, quality, or event relates to or connects with other things'; (c) the conscious but also unconscious levels of meanings, 'that involve structures, patterns, qualities, feelings, and emotions'; (d) the biological relation to its environment from both basic organic levels ('bottom-up') to more complex ones ('top-down'): 'The trick is to give a non-dualistic, embodied view of meaning that is not one-dimensional or reductivist'. Johnson's account clearly outlines the way in which Merleau-Ponty's account of meaning is broader and more inclusive: by identifying the body as the source of meaning, he has situated the question of meaning within the bigger existential dimension of human experience.

Intersubjectivity and communication

The problem of solipsism that had concerned Husserl in the *Cartesian Meditations* is the point of departure for Merleau-Ponty's analysis. Husserl attempted to establish the existence of the Other from the perspective of the self. But while the body of the Other, like that of the self, performs certain activities and displays its intentions, there is no way of knowing whether this Other is just a thing or another person. It is impossible, as Kwok-ying points out, to conceive of the Other 'who is at the same time a constituting subject and a constituted object' (2004: 140).

From the early *Phenomenology of Perception* to the unpublished *The Visible and the Invisible* Merleau-Ponty, the question of intersubjective relations was one that recurred throughout his writings. The continuity of the interest in this question shows that, as Moran (2013: 356) claims, there is no radical break between the earlier and later writings; what the later writing introduces is a new set of terms to bypass the latent Cartesian dualism still present in the *Phenomenology of Perception* where Merleau-Ponty acknowledges that '[t]he problems posed in [Phenomenology of Perception] are insoluble because I start there from the "consciousness"-"object" distinction' (1968: 200).

In *The Primacy of Perception* (1964), Merleau-Ponty contests the argument from the analogy that Husserl (as well as others) used to justify the existence of the Other. The need to justify the existence of the Other is derived from Cartesian-inflected psychology, with the mind posited as the private world of the self, a world that only it has access to so that, on these grounds, the self can only know the Other indirectly and itself directly. And the same argument applies to the analysis of the body: if the experiences of the body are sensory, these experiences are likewise also private. What can be concluded is that for both the mind and the body, the self and the Other are self-enclosed entities. The argument from analogy is used to justify the recognition of the Other as a projection from the self onto the Other because the Other has a body that is similar to that of the self. The problem with the argument from analogy is that it presupposes what it wants to prove. It is only because the self already knows what a body is that it can recognize the Other as having a human body and go on to infer that it also has a mind. Furthermore, Merleau-Ponty argues that the whole process of inferring the existence of a mind is a reflective process, but it is obvious that children recognize Others without going through any reflective process. Their experience of the Other as an embodied being is sufficient for them to understand immediately that the Other is an embodied being just like them.

Merleau-Ponty's position on the relation to the Other adopts a different point of departure. Instead of a self that knows itself introspectively, for Merleau-Ponty, what constitutes the self is an embodied openness towards the world and itself; just as the body of the self is a way of relating to the world, the body of the Other is also a way of relating to the world. The body of both the self and the Other are expressions of their intentions, and this mutual overlapping of bodily intentions is fundamental for his account as the '[i]t this transfer of my intentions to the other's body and of his intentions to my own [...] that make possible the perception of others' (1964: 118).

This is why Merleau-Ponty rejects the Husserlian emphasis on the transcendental ego as the methodological requirement by which to establish the existence of the Other. His central argument is that given our embodied subjectivity, to raise the question of solipsism is to ignore the existential and social dimension of human embeddedness. He dismisses solipsism as a doctrine on the grounds that it 'would strictly be true only of someone who managed to be tacitly aware of his existence without being anything and doing anything, which is impossible since existing is being in and of the world' (2002: 421). The argument for solipsism fails because human actions and behaviours can only be understood in relation to a world within which there are other humans who together co-constitute a world of significance. To argue for a shared world of significance, Merleau-Ponty adopts the Husserlian concept of pairing so as to claim that within the world, bodies are paired with Other bodies: self and Other are always mutually present. What the concept of pairing crucially reveals is that the body of the Other is not just a thing that can be understood in terms of mechanical or causal explanations but the body of a person whose actions are meaningful.

Merleau-Ponty calls the world in which the self and the Other share the 'prepersonal' world (2002: 405): it is the experience of the world that the self would call 'natural' because, before the notion of the self as a person arises, 'nature finds its way to the core of my personal life and becomes inextricably linked with it' (2002: 405). This is the natural way of being of both self and Other. At this primordial level of pre-personal embodied relations, at this 'pre-subjective modality of existence' (Coelho and Figueiredo 2003: 199), it is the body that constitutes the basis of meaningful intersubjective relations, a relationship that Merleau-Ponty describes as 'an anonymous existence':

> My life must have a significance which I do not constitute; there must strictly speaking be an intersubjectivity; each one of us must be both anonymous in the sense of the absolutely individual, and anonymous in the sense of absolutely general. Our being in the world is the concrete bearer of this double anonymity.
>
> (2002: 521)

Intersubjective relations constitute this 'double anonymity', and the world of lived experiences is one whereby the self and the Other are connected not through their rationality but through what Ying calls 'a relation of existence' (2004: 156). It is a world devoid of self-consciousness and one in which pre-linguistic communication takes place through the body, as typified by the actions and gestures used by young children to express themselves. The possibility of communication is derived from the body's 'indefinite power of giving significance – that is, both of apprehending and conveying a meaning' (Merleau-Ponty 2002: 226). In this pre-linguistic embodied domain of intersubjective relations, the question of solipsism does not occur. As such, there is a connection between bodies and a rudimentary form of communication whereby the self and Others express themselves through their bodies. This is why, despite the perceptual differences between self and Other, they both share a common world:

> In reality, the Other is not shut up inside my perspective of the world, because this perspective itself has no definite limits, because it slips spontaneously into the other's, and because both are brought together in the one single world in which we all participate as anonymous subjects of perception.
>
> (2002: 411)

As opposed to the Cartesian view of the subject as an isolated and solitary bearer of consciousness, Merleau-Ponty identifies consciousness with the body. Consciousness is embodied and situated within a world that contains other embodied consciousnesses: intersubjectivity is constituted by virtue of the relationships with Other bodies. To the question of how embodied consciousness interacts in the world, Merleau-Ponty introduces the concept of the chiasma to argue that bodily experiences are not private ones but interdependent with Other bodies. For example, the sensation of touch reveals that to have this sensation, it is not enough for the sensation to be experienced from the inside because it also requires something external that touches it: a hand both touches and is touched simultaneously. The same can be said of vision: 'he who sees cannot possess the visible unless he is possessed by it, unless he *is of it*' (1968: 134, original emphasis). There is a fundamental point being made: in the merging of the toucher and the touched, there is as yet no distinction between the subjective and the objective. At this level of lived experience, the body is both subject and object sharing in the pre-personal world of anonymous bodies. The sense of the subject as an autonomous being only arises after it is realized that the different experiences of the subject belong to one and the same body (1968: 141–42). But there is another step: from the pre-personal anonymous world of the body, the thought arises out of its interaction with the world and Others (1968: 143). The subject's sense of self only emerges in a secondary state when it starts to think about the world and Others. It is with the emergence of the subject as a self-conscious being that the question of the relationship with the Other arises. For Merleau-Ponty, solipsism is impossible because it is never possible for the self to be alone. In the pre-personal world, the self and the Other are entwined in the same anonymity, and it is only after the 'break' from the pre-personal and anonymous world that the question of solipsism becomes an issue:

> The solitude from which we emerge to intersubjective life is not that of the monads. It is only the haze of an anonymous life that separates us from being, and the barrier between us and others is impalpable. If there is a break, it is not between me and the other person; it is between a primordial generality we are intermingled in and the precise system, myself-the others.
>
> (1964b: 1743)

The problem of solipsism occurs, therefore, at a secondary stage of existence, one that is characterized by reflection and self-consciousness. This is why Merleau-Ponty discounts it as a problem because it is not one that arises as an existential concern. At the level of everyday existence, the self and the Oher interact with each other and within a world constituted of objects; it is in this world of significance that their actions can be mutually understood. The social world permeates the self and the Other: for Merleau-Ponty, the perception of the Other is not merely a projection of the self, for that would populate the world with multiple selves with no relation between them. But just as the self experiences the Other, the Other experiences the self: both share in this fundamental lived experience. This is why the idea underlying 'reflective' solipsism that the Other is 'isolated' and inaccessible is unwarranted. Solipsism would eliminate any form of communication between self and the Other: 'Solitude and communication cannot be the two horns of a dilemma but only two "moments" of one phenomenon since in fact other people do exist for me' (2002: 418).

As opposed to the idea of experiences being private, only accessible by the self, Merleau-Ponty counters by showing that what are considered private experiences are actively shared by others. Spoken language plays a crucial role in 'locking' the world of both self and Other because both belong to a shared world:

> [I]t suffices that [when] I look at a landscape, that I speak of it to someone. Then through the concordant operation of his body and my own what I see passes into him, this individual green of the meadow under my eyes invades his vision without quitting my own. I recognize in my green his green [...] There is no problem of the *alter ego* because it is not *I* who sees, not *he* who sees, because an anonymous visibility inhabits both of us, a vision in general.
>
> (1968: 142, original emphasis)

The common basis of bodies – of the self and the Other – is the world as the anonymous background that enables bodies to have experiences at all. Given that the embodied subject is situated within the world and that embodiment generates significance for all embodied subjects, intersubjective relations are the precondition for further communication. The communicative potential of the body provides an added crucial feature to human existence by making it possible to move beyond itself to reach out towards the world and Others. As embodied beings that are immersed in a world of significance, 'man [can] transcend[s] himself towards a new form of behaviour, or towards other people, or towards his own thought, through his body and his speech' (Merleau-Ponty 2002: 226) and this trajectory of significance is what constitutes a multi-layered argument against solipsism. At the perceptual level, the shared world is populated by other communicatively embodied subjects, and this is further amplified by the spoken word.

> Living language is precisely that togetherness of thinking and thing which causes the difficulty. In the act of speaking, the subject, in his tone and his style, bears witness to his autonomy, since nothing is more proper to him, and yet at the same moment, and without contradiction, he is turned towards the linguistic community and is dependent on his language, the will to speak is one and the same as the will to be understood. The presence of the individual in the institution and of the institution in the individual is evident in the case of linguistic change.
>
> (Merleau-Ponty 1970: 54–55)

In *Visible and the Invisible*, Merleau-Ponty suggests that the self–Other problem is 'a *Western* problem' (1968: 221, original emphasis), and while it might seem that he is alluding to other philosophical traditions, Moran (2013: 369) presumes that it refers to 'post-Cartesian modern philosophy', where the problem of the Other and the question of solipsism historically arises. For a number of philosophers, the problem of solipsism has shifted towards an examination of the relation between self and Others. For Sartre, for example, this relation is characterized by the gaze of the Other that transforms the self into a self-conscious being. More pertinent to the discussion here is the work of Levinas, who addresses Merleau-Ponty's account in 'On intersubjectivity: Notes on Merleau-Ponty' (1990) and 'Meaning and sense' (1996) For Levinas, despite Merleau-Ponty's framing of the self–Other relation at a corporeal level, he remains wedded to an epistemological framework because despite articulating the body as pre-theoretical it is still constituted from a theoretical position. On this account, the self–Other relation is one of mutual reciprocity, whereas, for Levinas, the relation is first and foremost asymmetrical, with the Other resisting any attempt to be reduced to an object. This refusal generates a sense of command and responsibility towards the Other operating prior to Being and consciousness in what he considers to be the primary ethical moment. For this reason, Levinas considers Merleau-Ponty's account as inadequate insofar as it fails to consider the primary ethical relations between self and Others by starting from subjective experience. In addition, it might also be argued that if what Merleau-Ponty brings to the question of the Other is a dialectical account of the self–Other relationship, as Low does (1992: 45–64), such that both are mutually implicated in the recognition of each other, then this implies a symmetrical relationship between them, precisely the point that Levinas is critical of.

However, in defence of Merleau-Ponty, Sanders (2008) argues that in *The Visible and the Invisible*, Merleau-Ponty's concept of reversibility that undoes the dichotomy between self and Others (as well as subject-object relations) should be understood along the same lines as Levinas' concept of the 'instant', i.e. the breaking out of pure Being into the subjectivity of the I. But, he adds that while Levinas' account focuses on the temporality of the self–Other relations, Merleau-Ponty's account of reversibility (and the flesh) introduces a spatial dimension to intersubjective relations as constituted along differences, and therefore not reducible to sameness as Levinas thinks.

Conclusion

The question of the Other and, therefore, of intersubjective relations is consistent throughout Merleau-Ponty's writings. With his account of the pre-personal world, he suggests an undifferentiated world in which lived bodies interact and communicate with each other and with the world. With the emergence of reflection and consciousness, the unity of the pre-personal world is eclipsed by the ossification of the self–Other and the self-world distinctions. By countering these distinctions, Merleau-Ponty's prioritization of embodied communication triangulates the relation of meaning between the self, the Other and the world, where each is always embedded in an interlocking network of meaning or significance. Merleau-Ponty's account of the embodied nature of human existence shows that the problem of solipsism – as Heidegger had also claimed in a different way – is a pseudo-problem. What is important about Merleau-Ponty's analysis of meaning from its prelinguistic gestural mode to its linguistic spoken dimensions is that the trajectory of meaning and communication is always already grounded in intersubjective relations.

3

Schutz and Habermas: From the Pure We-Relation to the Lifeworld

Introduction

Alfred Schutz is, within philosophical circles, not as well-known as he deserves to be, and this, perhaps, is in part because of the boundaries that disciplines tend to impose. But one quickly realizes the importance of his contributions to philosophical issues when one reads about his engagements with Hussserlian phenomenology, social theory, pragmatism, language and communication. The breadth of his writings itself warrants serious examination of his work. But one question he considers central to his writings is that of intersubjectivity. While his theory of intersubjectivity reveals that communication plays a key role in any account of intersubjectivity, the question that intrigues him is whether communication is the enabling condition for intersubjective relations or whether intersubjective relations are constituted prior to communication.

On the other hand, it would be a question of stating the obvious in highlighting the role of communication in Habermas's social philosophy, given that much of his insights are shaped by his 'linguistic turn'. However, having said this, it would be remiss to ignore him, given his prioritization of intersubjective relations in his critiques of subjectivity and consciousness. In effect, the role of communication is foundational since it provides the basis of social order insofar as it maintains and reproduces them while at the same time providing the resources that enable change to take place.

The common feature that ties Schutz and Habermas together is the value they attribute to language in their analysis of intersubjective relations and social life. In this chapter, I will first examine Schutz's critique of Husserl's account of intersubjectivity and follow it with an analysis of Schutz's account of the relation between communicative interaction within the lifeworld and its culmination in what he calls a 'pure We-Relation'. It will become apparent that while Schutz defends the priority of intersubjective relations, communicative interaction enables the richness of the lifeworld to be constituted. Likewise, in Habermas's account, communication always already presupposes a world of intersubjective relations. In this chapter I will first re-iterate his critique of subjectivity and, following this, elaborate on his account of intentionality and communication that is central to his account of the relationship between subjects in the lifeworld.

Schutz's critique of Husserl

Schutz discussed the question of intersubjectivity and Husserl's treatment of it in a number of papers, notably 'Scheler's theory of intersubjectivity and the general thesis of the alter ego' (1962) and 'The problem of transcendental intersubjectivity in Husserl' (1970). He was critical of Husserl's attempt to ground intersubjectivity by utilizing the method of transcendental phenomenology as elaborated upon in the *Cartesian Meditations*. The problem was that Husserl attempted to exclude everything that referred to others with his first phenomenological reduction, taking the transcendental subject as the foundation of sense. From here, he went on to claim that, following this exclusion, what was left was 'my own peculiar sphere' where only those experiences that belonged to the self or were 'owned' by the self were the ones that counted. As a result, it looked as though the transcendental self was trapped within its own world of meanings, a solipsistic world where everything else – the Others and nature – had no independence from the self. To overcome this problem, Husserl's approach to the constitution of the Other proceeded by adopting the methodological starting point of the 'exclusive ownness' of the self, arguing that the Other is constituted in two ways: (a) the (more basic) analogous constitution of the Other, where just as the self is constituted by an animate body with a consciousness, by analogy, the body of the Other is also an animate body with a consciousness; and (b) the associative constitution of the Other or 'pairing', where just as the self-pre-reflectively knows the world, in the same way, the Other pre-reflectively knows the world. There is a parallelism between self and Other that is constituted by a 'unity of similarity' (1999: 112–28).

Schutz expressed his dissatisfaction with Husserl's argument, claiming that the latter failed to explain how 'my transcendental ego can constitute in itself another transcendental ego' (1970: 54). He raises several objections against the Husserlian account:

(a) arguing that those experiences that did not belong or were not 'owned' by the ego could only be explained by acknowledging – as phenomenology does – the existence of an a priori world of intersubjective relations in, and through which, Others also conduct sense-making activities. 'All inference by analogy to Others' gestures already presuppose the psychical existence of the Others and our knowledge even of their experiences' (1962: 160);

(b) challenging the concept of pairing. Husserl had argued that just as the body of the self is paired with a consciousness, then if the body of the Other acted like that of a 'living body', the same would apply to the Other as a body with a consciousness. For Schutz, Husserl's position was flawed because 'he has not shown the possibility of a coexisting transcendental Alter Ego constituted within and by the activities of the transcendental ego. This, however, would be necessary in order to overcome the solipsistic argument in the transcendental spheres' (1962: 197). To ground intersubjectivity at a transcendental level, Husserl would need to account for the Other not only as it is presented in the natural attitude;

(c) criticizing Husserl's emphasis on the transcendental ego: if this ego bracketed the existence of the world and Others, then how is it possible to connect with the transcendental community that Husserl spoke about. By enclosing oneself in a solitary world of reflection, the opening towards the community is effectively shut:

> [E]ach transcendental ego has now constituted for himself, as to its being and sense, his world and in it all other subjects, including myself *but* he has constituted them *just for himself and not for all other transcendental egos as well.*
>
> (1970: 76, original emphasis)

In 'The Problem of Transcendental Intersubjectivity in Husserl' (1970: 51–84), Schutz's position is quite clear: rather than focus on intersubjectivity as something that needs to be constituted within the transcendental realm, it should be considered as a feature of the lifeworld. And it is in this respect that, despite the crucial contributions that Husserl's analysis provided, Schutz's position is 'superior' to that of Husserl (Trujillo 2018: 15).

Communication, intersubjectivity and the lifeworld

The analysis of everyday life, for Schutz, has the purpose of providing a theory of the social world; by using the resources provided by phenomenology, he can describe how humans experience the everyday world in a natural attitude. Intersubjective relations cannot be explained by reference to the constitutive activities of the transcendental ego but as an inherent feature of the lifeworld. Intersubjective relations are 'a datum of the life-world. It is the fundamental ontological category of human existence in the world' (1970: 82). Given that the relation between self and Other is grounded in a specific spatio-temporal context, this reinforces Schutz's claim that the lifeworld is 'not my private world but from the beginning an intersubjective one common to all. intersubjective from the very beginning' (1962: 167).

The theory of the lifeworld is developed in *Collected Papers 1: The Problem of Social Reality* (1962), and it is the everyday world as experienced in the natural attitude by adults. It is the world that is taken for granted, the world that the self is conscious of and within which their actions unfold motivated by pragmatic concerns. Schultz also calls it the 'paramount reality', and within this reality, the self acts upon both objects and Others in the world, and these, in turn, influence the self, at times obliging them to change their actions (1962: 277-8). In a number of instances, Schutz acknowledges the centrality of the role of language in the interrelation between intersubjectivity and the lifeworld, describing it as 'the paramount vehicle for communication' (1976: 160).

The importance of the lifeworld is that it describes life prior to theory: it is the world of experiences within which both the self and the Other live their lives. The focus on the world as it is experienced brings out his disagreement with Husserl's approach, whose phenomenological method had as its goal the discovery of the invariant structures of a socio-historical world (Schutz 1962: 278). To answer the question of how social life has the meaning it does, Schutz takes the first-person experience of the world as a point of departure. The self experiences the world meaningfully and assumes that the Other also experiences the world meaningfully.

> I assume everything which has meaning for me also has meaning for the Other or Others with whom I share this, my life-world [...] This life-world presents itself also to them for interpretation, [...] I posit meaningful acts in the expectation that Others will interpret them meaningfully, and my schema of positing is oriented with respect to the Others' schema of interpretation. [...] on these reciprocal acts of positing meaning and of interpretation of meaning, my social world of mundane intersubjectivity is built; it is also the social world of Others, and all other social and cultural phenomena are founded upon it.
>
> (Schutz 1962: 135)

Schultz introduces the distinction between the 'in-order-to' and the 'because motive' to explain the meaning of human actions (1962: 218). This distinction allows him to show the reasons people give for their actions. The 'in-order-to' motivation of action is future and goal-oriented as it explains why the self is performing a particular action at the present moment (such as walking to the post office). The 'because motive' is the retrospective explanation of an action after it has been performed (because I wanted to buy stamps). While the meaning of the 'in-order-to' motivations is subjective, the 'because' motivations are objective. This distinction is important because it provides a theoretical framework for understanding actions as they are experienced pragmatically in the lifeworld.

It should be pointed out that there is a distinction to be made between the pragmatic dimension of intersubjectivity and the lifeworld per se; they are not identical insofar as the pragmatic dimension is narrower. The pragmatic world is the world of action within which persons live their lives going about their affairs and which, in the course of their interactions, establish relationships with Others, the establishment of which requires that they understand each other. What characterizes the pragmatic dimension, for him, is the immediate and direct presence of the Other in a face-to-face relationship (our 'consociates') with whom the same spatio-temporal space is shared, where the uniqueness of each individual is open to the Other and where intentions are mutually expressed together with the possibility of feedback in the cases of misunderstanding. Schutz considers this to be the primary mode of being of intersubjective relationships in the lifeworld, although this needs to be qualified insofar as the face-to-face is not necessarily the space of intimacy as it can include both friends and strangers (Zaner 1961: 81).

On the other hand, the concept of the lifeworld is broader because while the face-to-face is direct in its relations with Others, it is possible to relate to Others indirectly, to have relationships that are not grounded in the immediacy of the present and its shared spatio-temporal location. To account for these Other relationships, Schutz introduces three categories: our contemporaries, predecessors and successors. Our contemporaries exist simultaneously with us but are not spatially present; they can include individuals, groups and abstract social entities with whom one might interact. As can be imagined within the class of contemporaries, there is a lot of variation and degrees of interaction. Our predecessors existed in the past before our birth, and although their relation to us is indirect as they are not part of our temporal world, what they produced influences us in the present. And our successors will exist in the future after our death; they cannot influence us as they do not exist yet, while what we do now can affect them. Crossley (1996: 92) raises an interesting point, in that while successors belong to a future that we do not know about, this does not entail neglecting the moral relation we have to those who will follow us, taking care of the environment, for example, is something that we owe to our successors.

In addition, there are other indirect ways the self relates to Others: through what they have left behind, through their products. There are a whole range of objects, images and symbols that are part and parcel of the fabric of the lifeworld that are not constituted within the current spatio-temporal situation. We know about them because there are 'traces' or signs of the past presence of Others that continue to permeate the present. The meaning of these products can only be understood with reference to – as Schutz points out, invoking Weber – the 'subjective meaning' of the humans who produced them. The lifeworld is the background prepared by Others that gives the present meaning and a sense of direction: it is 'socially derived, and transmitted to the individual in the long process of education by parents, teachers, teachers of teachers' (1962: 120).

The meaningfulness of actions within the lifeworld is constituted by what Schutz calls the 'stock of knowledge' that is inherited, learned and presupposed by its members. From the experience of the first person, different individuals, each with their own experiences, construct types that have something in common for all who share in this experience. The type is the shared meaning: in effect, the experience is transformed into a social construct, into a type that is linguistically named and consolidated, and it is this that the individual learns by living with Others within the lifeworld. The movement from a particular individual to Others generates intersubjective social knowledge: it is a knowledge of types ('strangers' or 'dogs') that enable the self to navigate its way in the world. This, in turn, contributes to the 'accumulation' of knowledge that informs the lifeworld.

Communication plays a crucial role in both consolidating and furthering intersubjective relations. Recognizing the Other as other enables the creation of a 'communicative common environment' (Schutz 1962: 27), which in turn feeds into the lifeworld generating more sophisticated typifications (1962). The lifeworld consists of the accumulation of those experiences that, over time, have been transformed into knowledge and transmitted through the process of socialization to the individual who uses this knowledge to navigate around their social world.

In addition to the 'paramount reality' of the lifeworld, there are, nested within it, other 'finite provinces of meaning' (1962: 230ff) and other forms of reality that enable the self to transcend their everyday life. Given that each of these worlds constitutes an enclave of meaning, the question Schutz tackles is how to connect these multiple realities together. This is where his theory of signs and symbols as forms of communication becomes pivotal, enabling the experience of these worlds to be communicated to others. The role of signs in communication is that, for Schutz, of expressing the mental contents of the Other (1989: 257), and they are used pragmatically for the attainment of practical goals in the context of everyday life. They are the medium that establishes relationships within 'paramount reality' (1971: 252–54). While there is a difference between signs and symbols, what they both have in common is that they involve 'transcendences': in the case of signs, their use entails transcending oneself and connecting with Others; in the case of symbols, communication transcends the everyday world, whether it involves the private world of the person – their fantasies and dreams – or whether it is institutional – as in political, religion, science and art (1989: 290).

To explain the ways signs and symbols function, Schutz adopts the Husserlian concept of appresentation. However, while Husserl restricted the application of this concept to establish the intersubjective domain, Schutz extends its range of application to other domains of meaning through the use of signs and symbols. Signs, and perhaps the most important of these are linguistic signs, consist of a sound paired with a sense. However, communication with the everyday world does not only take place through signs but also through symbols. With symbols, a visible object presents 'an idea which transcends our experience of everyday life' (1962: 331). Through analogical appresentation, the perception of an object might lead to the presentation of another object, with the object defined broadly to include memories, fantasies and fiction (1962: 294ff). The importance of symbolic appresentation is that it establishes a connection between the everyday world and the various other domains of meaning (1962: 343). Because symbols are understood and shared they perform a unifying role in society. Dreher sums up the importance of the symbol: '[T]hrough symbols the multiple realities are represented within the reality of everyday life and through communication these realities can become intersubjective and objectified and therefore can influence action' (2003: 143).

The centrality of communication in articulating the lifeworld is evident in that it is the 'gel' that enables the movement across the various domains of meaning in the lifeworld. Communication bridges the everyday world of paramount reality and the multiple realities that together constitute the lifeworld: '[t]he world of everyday life, of everyday experience, has a paramount position above other provinces of reality, *since only within it does communication with our fellowmen become possible*' (Schutz 1989: 244, original emphasis).

The pure We-Relation

In his analysis of intersubjective relations within the lifeworld, Schutz breaks down these relations into their most fundamental elements, into what he calls the pure We-Relationship, whereby humans relate to each other as living, thinking and communicating beings (1974: 64). The pure We-Relationship is the prior condition for both communication as well as for the interaction within the lifeworld (1970: 82).

To account for how it is possible to have intersubjective relations, the key for Schutz is establishing how the self and the Other create meaningfulness and, crucially, how this meaning connects both. Starting from the phenomenological account of experience, Schutz writes:

> If we simply live immersed in the flow of duration, we encounter only undifferentiated experiences that melt into one another in a flowing continuum [...] However,

> when, by my act of reflection, I turn my attention to my living experience, I am no longer taking up my position within the stream of duration [...] The experiences which were constituted as phases within the flow of duration now become objects of attention as constituted experiences.
>
> (1967: 51)

Central to Schultz's account of the meaningfulness of experience is his distinction between the domain of life, of 'lived experience' and the domain of thought, of reflection. Life unfolds in what he calls the 'inner time' of consciousness whereby the self is immersed in its experiences: this is a state that is internal to the self and opposed to the externality of thought, which focuses outwardly on objects, including oneself as an 'object' in the world. What this distinction brings out is that the self first experiences life and only after, at a secondary level, reflects upon it. Given that thought occurs after the actual experience, then the reflection is about something past, something that has already happened. The role of thought is important for it transforms the experience that unfolds within the self's stream of consciousness at a pre-phenomenal level into a meaningful experience at a phenomenal level. Once thought reflects upon one's specific behaviour, it becomes a phenomenal segment that differentiates it from the rest of the self's behaviour. Grinnell (1983: 186–87) raises two points: (a) the self does not experience itself as behaving because its experiences move seamlessly from one to the Other; it is thought that abstracts from these experiences so as to reflect upon the behaviour once it has passed; (b) it is because the behaviour has become phenomenal, that it is now meaningful. It is the self in its sense-making function that projects meaning onto the behaviour: '[t]he meaning is the *way* in which the Ego regards this experience. The meaning lies in the attitude of the Ego toward that part of its stream of consciousness which has already flowed by' (Schutz 1967: 69–70, original emphasis).

The question now shifts to the Other whose experience mirrors that of the self: 'simultaneous with *my* lived experience of you, there is *your* lived experience which belongs to you and is part of your stream of consciousness' (1967: 108, original emphasis). The fundamental question for understanding social relations from a phenomenological position is how one moves from the domain of the 'solitary consciousness' to the Other. Schutz establishes the existence of the Other through the use of appresentation. The appresentation of the Other starts with the experience of the Other as it is given to the self: the self perceives a body that it couples, or that is appresented with a mind, in the same way as the self is constituted as a body with a mind; this process of coupling or appresentation is not inferred but automatic. However, it is not just a question of mutual perception between self and Other, but, in addition, that the Other also perceives its own body in the same way as the self does. Consequently, the body of the Other cannot be considered as constituted by the self but as an 'organism, not of my mind but of an Other's mind'. This enables Schutz to justify the claim of what he calls 'the general thesis of the alter ego's existence'.

Having established the existence of the Other as an independent body with its own stream of consciousness, how do these two streams of consciousness interact? His answer points to the parallelism in the structure of consciousness of both the self and the Other: the

> stream of thought which is not mine, shows the same fundamental structure as my own consciousness. This means that the Other is like me, capable of acting and thinking; that his stream of thought shows the same through and through connectedness as mine; that analogous to my own life of consciousness this shows the same time structure [...]; that consequently, he has the genuine experience of growing old with me as I know that I do with him.
>
> (Schutz 1962: 174)

For Schutz, this 'mutual tuning-in' is what constitutes the foundation of intersubjective relations as a 'pure We-Relation' with the self and Other sharing the same space and time in a face-to-face relation where the self's consciousness directed or intends the Other and vice-versa.

Zaner (1961: 82) elaborates on the 'three moments' involved in the 'mutual tuning-in' as it develops into a communicative exchange: (a) the speaker articulates their thoughts mentally and expresses them linguistically through their bodies with the listener understanding and re-iterating these thoughts in their minds; (b) this communicative exchange unfolds externally in a face-to-face relation; (c) the We-Relation as face-to-face is the precondition for their being a communicative exchange that goes beyond the uniqueness of each individual, i.e. their biography. The face-to-face feature of the We-Relation is the foundation of intersubjective relation as '"the mutual tuning-in relationship", upon which alone all communication is founded' (Schutz 1976: 161).

It might seem that, as Lachowska (1980) points out, two different senses of meaning are being used. On the one hand, meaning occurs with reflection, but on the other hand, meaning is always already inherent in our relations to Others. For her, the latter is the stronger case for in our relations to Others, certain mutually agreed upon expectations of them arise such that, for example, one expects a shop assistant to behave in a certain way towards you, and this is not just a subjective expectation. Furthermore, the priority of the world of intersubjective relations over that of a world of the solitary subject is entailed by the nature of language itself: as Schutz points out,

> [t]he vernacular of everyday life is primarily a language of named things and events, and any name includes a typification and generalisation referring to the relevance

> system prevailing in the linguistic in-group which found the named thing significant enough to provide a separate term for it.
>
> (1962: 14)

The question of intersubjectivity is one of the fundamental questions that Schutz engaged with. While his point of departure was Husserl's transcendental-phenomenological attempt to ground intersubjectivity in the constitutive consciousness of the self, Schutz's analysis moves away from consciousness to ground intersubjectivity as the way of being in the lifeworld. And crucially, as I have shown, for Schutz, not only is communication essential to the lifeworld, but it itself presupposes intersubjective relations.

Habermas on the interrelation between communication and intersubjectivity: The critique of the subject

Habermas's overarching interests can be broadly divided into, firstly, his critical examination of modern society that has led to a number of disturbing features, such as the increasing alliance between capitalism and the state, as well as the increasing domination of everyday life by technology and the disaffection and decline of public participation in politics; secondly, his work has a more interventionist angle in that he examines what is entailed by processes of communication as well as how these processes contribute to questions of morality, law and politics. Although it can be said that there is a continuity between both interests, I will be focusing chiefly on the second of these and, in particular, on the question of why the possibility of communication itself presupposes rules that have been agreed upon by subjects who are always already situated within a lifeworld constituted by intersubjective relations. To this end, I will rely chiefly on one of his most influential texts, *The Theory of Communicative Action*, and supplement it with *On the Pragmatics of Communication* and *On the Pragmatics of Interaction*.

One underlying and continual theme throughout Habermas's writings is his critique of the philosophy of the subject, or consciousness, as the point of departure for any social philosophy, with his theory of communicative action providing the theoretical resources for conducting this critique. In *The Philosophical Discourse of Modernity* (1990a), he traces the genealogy of subjectivity and consciousness in western philosophy to show how pervasive it has become, labelling it as a 'paradigm' for modern as well as postmodern philosophy. This shift towards the subject can be traced to the Cartesian subject-object dichotomy, where the subject was posited over and above, and in opposition, to the world of objects and nature. The subject was characterized by self-consciousness with the capacity to act freely and opposed to an objective, non-self-conscious nature that proceeded mechanically according to its laws. By focusing on the subject as an isolated individual, Habermas points out that a number of problems were generated: epistemologically, knowledge of the subject becomes possible if the subject is treated as an object and studied from the third-person position; linguistically, meaning is restricted to the interior world of the subject with its role as representing (mentally) the external world, dislocated from its everyday communicative function; socially, the individual is likened to an atom existing apart from and without any essential relation to Others. These different forms of subjectivity are essentially 'monological' in that they all presuppose a solitary subject. For Habermas, the problems mentioned above neglect the centrality of dialogue as the communicative model that highlights the priority of intersubjective relations.

In *On the Pragmatics of Social Interaction* (2001), Habermas extends his critique of the philosophy of the subject towards what he calls the 'constitutive theories' of society. The key word here is 'constitutive': just as Kant argued that the condition of possibility of the experience of nature lay in the constitutive power of the transcendental subject, social theorists adopted this perspective but shifted the constitutive power away from the subject to society as a whole. The major difference between Kant and later social theorists was that while for Kant, the possibility of the experience of nature was a cognitive activity, social theorists considered social life as constituted through ordinary practices of everyday life. The problem for Habermas is that these theories fail to appreciate the extent of the relationships between subjects in everyday life; they neglect the extent to which communicative interaction is the gel that brings together social reality.

This is why, for Habermas, language plays a pivotal account in his theory of communicative action: '[l]anguage is the ground of intersubjectivity, and every person must have set foot on it before he can objectivate himself in his first expression of life, whether in words, attitudes, or actions' (1972: 157). The possibility of human social existence is predicated upon linguistic communication insofar as it enables 'autonomy and responsibility' as well as by establishing intersubjective relations through its performativity. For Habermas, 'only those expressions that can be *expanded* into explicit speech-acts come into consideration' (1982: 270, original emphasis) since these serve to coordinate actions. But the emphasis on linguistic communication has been criticized, and in particular on speech acts, fails to take into consideration (a) that there are other non-linguistic forms of communication, such as those expressed through art or through the action itself, and (b) the emphasis on speech-acts as literal forms of communication ignores other forms of linguistic communication such as 'irony, metaphor or multivocity [...] poetic or satiric speech [...] artistic constructions that communicate, with political cueing or wordless judgements, with editorials or rhetorical ingenuity' (Vejera 1986: 86).

However, Habermas's valorization of linguistic communication is understandable, given his critique of the philosophy of the subject. In order to establish a critical social theory, he suggests that linguistic communication – in its performative and normative dimensions – provides the theoretical resources for this theory. While not all actions in society are spoken, in 'What is Universal Pragmatics?' (1979: 1–68), he prioritizes verbal intersubjective communication as the key to explaining how subjects interact in society. Communicative action aims to enable understanding between subjects, and this is best done with language: '[r]eaching understanding is the inherent telos of human speech' (1984: 287).

The predominance of linguistic communication in Habermas's thinking can be justified by considering his overarching project of establishing a critical theory of society. Edgar points out, '[w]hile it [universal pragmatics] does indeed explain the constitution of social relations through communicative competence, it also provides a critical resource through which illegitimate forms of social organisation may be recognised' (2005: 153). By being able to understand each other through linguistic communication, subjects are both able to coordinate their actions in society as well as challenge any abuses that are taking place. This is the way his theory of communicative action and his theory of society are aligned. With his theory of universal pragmatics, Habermas sought to provide an account (a) that reconstructs the competences with which speakers can communicate, and (b) of how speakers communicate in everyday life to produce a relatively stable social life.

Habermas is interested in how rules constitute the intersubjective nature of social reality and, in particular, how linguistic rules are used by competent subjects to communicate. In this respect, Chomsky's 'deep grammar' demonstrated how speakers competently follow the rules of language, producing meaningful utterances, even though they are unaware of them. While Chomsky's project was narrower in that he strove to discover the rules that enable speakers to use language, Habermas's universal pragmatics is broader in that it attempts to discover the competence required to follow such rules within a social dimension.

Habermas utilizes the writings of speech act theorists J. L. Austin and J. Searle so as to transform universal pragmatics into a social theory. The relation between subjects is created by virtue of the speech acts (1979: 30–32) used within a context. Within a military context, a command establishes a relationship between the commanding officer and the soldier; within the library, a request for a book establishes a relationship between a student and a librarian. However, it is from Wittgenstein's later writings, that Habermas finds the theoretical resources for the elaboration of universal pragmatics. The degree to which he has taken up Wittgenstein's concept of language games is such that universal pragmatics might be called 'a general theory of language games' (Burleson and Kline 1979: 415). The analogy with Wittgenstein's language games brings home the point concerning the centrality of rules and competences. Just as playing a game entails that the player is competent in following the rules of the game – despite perhaps not being able to explain those rules – a competent language user can use language by following the rules without necessarily knowing them. In addition, despite being bound by the rules, it is possible to react creatively to situations one has not previously experienced. This applies to playing games and to language where one can understand an utterance even if one has never heard it before. The importance of linguistic (and non-linguistic) rules is that they are socially agreed upon. A rule cannot be followed by one person, an argument celebrated as Wittgenstein's critique of the private language argument. The rules of language are public and, therefore, provide an objective way of eliminating arbitrary use of words.

There is a further idea that Habermas finds significant: for the later Wittgenstein, the role of language is not merely that of picturing a non-linguistic reality by forming sentences to represent that reality. Instead, what is interesting for Wittgenstein is the way speakers use the same linguistic rules in different contexts; language use becomes a question of appropriateness, of knowing how to use the specific rules of language according to the various contexts. A competent speaker knows which rules are appropriate for each context such that the speaker also knows which utterances do not belong to a specific language game. This explains why the utterances within religious communication differ from those of poetry or science. Here is a further elaboration of the difference between Habermas and Chomsky: for the latter competence was 'merely' a matter of generating the right utterances, but for the former, communication entails the speaker generating the right utterances within a specific context: 'in order to participate in normal discourse, the speaker must have at his disposal, in addition to his linguistic competence, basic qualifications of speech and symbolic interaction (role-behaviour), which we may call *communicative* competence' (Habermas 2008: 367, original emphasis).

Communication and intention

Despite the importance of the later Wittgenstein, Habermas points out that while his insight into the intersubjective dimension of language use between social subjects cannot be underestimated, his account remains problematic because (a) his views come across as promoting a context-relative view where within each context, there is an intersubjective agreement on the use of such rules, but that these rules are incommensurable across various contexts. It suggests that subjects live together in a linguistic 'bubble' detached from other contexts and well as from a non-linguistic reality. For Habermas, the goal of universal pragmatics is that of reconstructing what is common to all language users, and by articulating the competences of all speakers over and above their specific contexts, he can claim that his project is universal in scope; and (b) his concept of language-games does not allow speakers to challenge the rules of their language-games. Given that Habermas wants to insert a critical dimension to the concept of language games, he argues (2001: 61) that there is a 'double structure' to ordinary language that accounts for the relationship that necessarily obtains between competent speakers, i.e. their intersubjective relations and the content of what it is that they are communicating.

The distinction between the illocutionary force, i.e. the intentions of speakers, and the propositional content of utterances, i.e. what the utterance is referring to, is reconfigured by Habermas in his articulation of the 'double structure' of language: every utterance, on his account, has both features but, according to the type of utterance being used, one is predominant. With cognitive utterances, the focus is primarily on the truth or falsity of the content, while at a secondary level, a relation between subjects is also established. With normative utterances, the focus is principally on the intersubjective dimension of the utterance, with the cognitive aspect taking a secondary role. Communicative action entails understanding both the intentions of the speaker in producing the utterance as well as what the utterance is about and the important point is that just as a cognitive utterance can be challenged both for its factual information and appropriateness, so too a normative utterance can be challenged for both its appropriateness and its content. It has been pointed out that the details of Habermas's linguistics suffer from the problem of being 'underdeveloped' insofar as he only provides 'general suggestions' concerning the grammatical structures and forms of expression, and while a detailed account of the linguistics aspect might not be necessary for his critical theory, it becomes 'impossible to assess adequately the utility and fruitfulness of this theory given its present unelaborated state' (Burleson and Kline 1979: 416).

The emphasis on the communicative intent of speakers explains why Habermas prioritizes linguistic actions. While not all actions are linguistic, and the terminology of communicative action seems to exclude non-linguistic actions, he is chiefly interested in those communicative acts that express the intentions of speakers and by defining communication as mutual understanding, he argues that when subjects understand each other, they understand the intentions speakers had in uttering what they did.

Communicative action entails that speakers understand what it is that the Other intends them to do through their utterances. This enables Habermas to differentiate between communicative action and strategic action. Communicative action is opposed to both strategic action (actions involving the social world) and instrumental action (actions involving the natural world). Strategic communication, while parasitic on everyday communication, differs in that it involves the duplicity of speakers as they mask their intentions, and rather than communicating to achieve mutual understanding, they communicate with the goal of achieving their ends successfully; while this is appropriate for certain endeavours, such as games, when it is used in intersubjective relations, it becomes manipulative for the Other is treated as an object, as a means to an end (1982: 263–64). The way towards achieving a goal is framed along the distinction between understanding and consent on the one hand and causality and influence on the Other in the way actions are achieved; for the former, participants discuss and arrive at an understanding and agreement on the action that is good for all, while with the latter, strategies are used to influence others into doing what is, in effect, good for oneself (2002: 203). As Rasor comments, '[w]hen individuals act out of a goal-oriented or instrumental orientation, the shared social lifeworld is eventually destroyed. This is what Habermas seeks to avoid by his emphasis on intersubjective or communicative orientation' (2000: 278).

This distinction reinforces Habermas's critique of the philosophy of the subject since strategic actions are oriented towards the interest of the solitary subject. Strategic actions entail that the self masks their intentions: this can be seen in certain games (poker, chess) where in order to win the game, competent players must be strategic in their actions, not revealing their intentions. The example from games serves to highlight another point: if a player makes a wrong move in a game because they did not realize they were breaking a rule, then the play is halted so that the rule can be explained, and it resumes once the player understands what they did wrong. But when there is a communication breakdown, there is no halt to linguistic communication and no suspension of language because it is only through language that the breakdown can be resolved. As Habermas points out, language can turn on itself; it is reflexive (2001: 73), and a competent speaker can establish relations with other subjects and use language's meta-linguistic resources to 'fix' communication when it breaks down. Habermas (2001: 138) uses the example of a child to illustrate his point: when a child starts saying 'No' to its mother, this constitutes a crucial stage in the child's development insofar as it has recognized the mother's intentions and challenges them. The child has learnt that both the mother and itself are social agents expressing their intentions, and by refusing to obey its mother's commands, it has expressed its intentions with the resultant breakdown in communication. It is only when the mother provides explanations to the child that the breakdown is resolved.

The concept of illocutionary force is particularly important for Habermas because it shows how the success of a speech act creates the context within which utterances have the force to bring subjects together, by so doing establishing relationships between them. Habermas, like Derrida, is interested in how speech acts create contexts instead of institutionally defined contexts (such as the Church or the military) (2001: 82–83).

Intersubjective communication is rationally grounded in Habermas's concept of validity claims, where any challenges to utterances can be resolved through rational argumentation. Participants must be able to justify what they say by providing reasons for their claims. The term 'validity claims' is self-explanatory: any claim made by a speaker must be defended if it is challenged by someone else. Their centrality in Habermas's project is that they constitute what is common to all speech; in other words, their universality enables speakers to become competent communicative subjects who can establish and maintain social relations.

There are four types of claims (2001: 63–64) that a speaker must be able to validate. They are claims to

(1) Intelligibility: these concern the sense or meaning of the claim,
(2) Truth: these concern the truth or falsity of the claim,
(3) Rightfulness: these concern the appropriateness of speakers in making the claim,
(4) Truthfulness: these concern the intentions and sincerity of the speaker of the claim.

Aside from the first claim oriented towards the medium of language, all the other claims establish a relation to the external world, the social world and the inner world.

> If the intelligibility of an utterance becomes problematic, we ask such questions as, 'What do you mean by that?' 'How am I to understand that?' 'What does that mean?' We call answers to such questions *interpretations*. If the truth of the propositional content of an utterance becomes problematic, we ask such questions as 'Are things as you say?' 'Why are they that way and not some other way?' We reply to such questions with *assertions* and *explanations*. If the normative rightness of a speech act or its normative context becomes problematic, we ask such questions as, 'Why did you do that?' 'Why didn't you behave differently?' To these questions we respond with *justifications*. Finally, if in the context of an interaction we call into doubt another's sincerity we ask questions such as, 'Is he deceiving me?' or 'Is she deceiving herself about herself?'.
>
> (2001: 90–91, original emphasis)

In the aforementioned communicative situations, any 'breakdown' in communication can only be resolved through further communication. However, the validity claims that enable these communicative breakdowns to be resolved differ, and Habermas (2001: 91) separates them into two groups:

(a) problems with the claims to intelligibility and truthfulness: with cases of intelligibility, when the meaning of the utterance is challenged, speakers resort to repeating what they say using other words; if the difficulty is more complex (as with literary texts), speakers engage in 'hermeneutic' practices, asking for explanations at a meta-communicative level. In the case of truthfulness, when the sincerity of the speech act is challenged, its redemption can only be made by examining the behaviour of the speaker in relation to what the speaker has said (do they keep their promises); the meta-communicative level involves examining the relation between what a person says and what they do with very serious cases of insincerity leading to professional help. These two validity claims differ insofar as no reasons can be provided to justify the claims.

(b) problems with truth and normative claims: these are resolved by shifting the debate to the level of discourse. With the concept of discourse, Habermas introduces the idea that the resolution of these problems occurs when the speaker's claims are subjected to critical interrogation by the participants and accepted or rejected on the basis of what he calls 'the force of the better argument'. Given that participants aim at achieving an understanding as a result of their argumentation, the pragmatic or cogency of the argument becomes the criteria for accepting the truth or normativity of a claim. Inbuilt within the structure of discourse is the assumption that speakers can provide reasons or justifications for holding the beliefs or norms they do. Habermas describes inherited rationality within everyday intersubjective communication as the 'supposition of mutual accountability', though what is entailed by this 'supposition' is debatable.

It is clear from the way rational (truth-related) and practical (norm-related) discourses unfold in everyday life that there is a gulf between what actually happens and Habermas's theoretical reconstruction of communicative interaction. To account for this discrepancy, he introduces the concept of the 'ideal speech situation', defined as 'a speech situation in which communications not only are not impeded by external contingent influences, but also not by constraints resulting from the structure of communication itself. The ideal speech situation excludes systematic distortion of communication' (2001: 97–98).

Habermas claims that the 'ideal speech situation' is a regulative ideal in that it highlights the conditions that need to be met for intersubjective communication to take place. There are four conditions: the first set of conditions involves the equality of participants (a) who have an equal opportunity for commencing and continuing discourse and (b) who have an equal opportunity in deploying constative speech acts (challenging, asserting, explanation, etc.). The second set of conditions concerns the equality of participants: (c) who are free to express their personal lives by communicating their intentions and feelings and (d) who are entitled to assume the power that goes with regulative speech acts, such as for example, commanding. Burleson and Kline point out, these enabling conditions are 'the constitutive conditions for all intersubjective communication' (1979: 424) because if one did not assume that participants are equal and free in their communicative interactions, they would not bother participating in discourse. The possibility for a rational consensus can be attained when all these conditions are met.

The prioritization of the social and the linguistic in Habermas's philosophy might lead one to think that the self is merely a reflection of the social in its formation. While this might be the point of departure in the formation of the identity of the self, Habermas adopts Mead's I-Me distinction such that the self emerges as it learns the competences required to participate in society. Communicative competence 'permits the individual to internalise conventional norms and employ them in appropriate contexts' (Rasor 2000: 284). As a result of this process, the self acquires a moral identity. The connection between moral development and social evolution is a theme that Habermas explores in *Communication and the Evolution of Society* (1979), arguing that while acquiring the competence to participate socially and morally in society belongs to the conventional stage, in a post-conventional stage, the self expresses itself as an individual by being able to adopt a critical stand towards its society by appealing to a higher principle, to what he calls a universal communication community.

In *Moral Consciousness and Communicative Action* (1990b), Habermas introduces the concept of discourse ethics that retrains the framework of the theory of communicative action but narrows the focus to the domain of human relationships, which are implicitly characterized by moral rules. Discourse ethics comes into being when participants disagree on certain norms and rationally discuss the validity of the claims being made. Whereas the earlier communicative ethics focused on issues of Marxism and ideology, the later ethics deals with questions of justice. What changes with discourse ethics is that the earlier presuppositions entailed by competent speakers are now renamed as the rules of discourse. These rules are:

1. Every subject with the competence to speak and act is allowed to take part in a discourse.

2a. Everyone is allowed to question any assertion whatever.

2b. Everyone is allowed to introduce any assertion whatever into the discourse.

2c. Everyone is allowed to express his attitudes, desires and needs.
3. No speaker may be prevented, by internal or external coercion, from exercising his rights as laid down in (1) and (2) (1990b: 89).

There are two principles underlying Habermas's theory of discourse ethics: these are the principle of Universalization (U) and the principle of discourse (D). In the case of (U), the principle of universalization is presupposed by all who engage in an ethical debate; in other words, when a speaker presents an argument, they assume that what is being argued for must be acceptable to all for it to carry weight, and not just to themselves (1990b: 65). This is why since the norm that has been chosen in ethical debates would have an effect on the lives of others, it must be clear why one norm and not another has been chosen. In the case of (D), Habermas argues that the way to justify the validity of norms is through intersubjective communication. Although the influence of Kant is evident in his adoption of the principle of universalism (U), he opposes the Kantian model of morality insofar as the Kantian moral agent thinks of norms on their own, i.e. as a monological reasoner. But for Habermas, dialogue is crucial to discourse ethics because 'only those norms can claim to be valid that meet (or could meet) with the approval of all affected in their *capacity as participants in a practical discourse*' (1990b: 66, original emphasis).

Habermas's discourse ethics has three key features: it is cognitive, universal, and formal (1990b: 120–21). By cognitive, he argues that by providing reasons and arguments, ethical judgements can be grounded 'objectively' as opposed to those theories that reduce ethics to expressions of the subjectivity of taste (and therefore beyond discussion). By 'universalism', he counters the cultural relativism that is associated with ethical theories by arguing that ethical discussion can be evaluated on the basis of which argument has the better force. By 'formalism', he avoids positioning himself as telling others what they ought to do with their lives. Discourse ethics is only concerned with the procedures for solving moral problems rather than providing solutions. It is not a substantive ethic with prescriptions on how to live one's life but a theory that recognizes the ongoing process of validating one's moral values and ensuring that ethical debates are conducted fairly. In opposition to Rawls, discourse ethics shows that moral discourse unfolds as an intersubjective relation between subjects engaged in a dialogical argument.

Intersubjectivity and the lifeworld

The subjects who engage and communicate with each other are not dislocated or abstract beings but, as humans, they bring with them all those features that identify them as particular persons situated within a specific context and within which they interact dialogically. Habermas uses the terminology of the lifeworld derived from Husserl and Schutz to account for the resources that enable the subject to act competently. However, he develops his analysis to move beyond their phenomenological focus on the subject of experience by broadening his account to include both linguistic and intersubjective relations within the lifeworld: 'Communicative action takes place within a lifeworld that remains at the back of participants in communication. It is present to them only in the prereflective form of taken-for-granted background assumptions and naively mastered skills' (1984: 335). The centrality of the lifeworld for Habermas is that it enables him to connect the theory of communicative action with the theory of society by explaining the way a society reproduces itself by providing the resources for both social integration and critical discussion (1984: 370).

Given that the lifeworld consists of those assumptions that subjects take for granted, that enables them to understand what is happening in specific situations, it is also the space within which changes become possible. In this sense, the lifeworld is malleable because it shows how those norms that are taken for granted within a society can change through the interaction of its members. To highlight the particularities that are taken for granted in the lifeworld, Habermas narrates the story of a construction site with an older worker sending the new younger one to buy beer for their break. The problem between them arises because, while for an older worker, this is an accepted practice (delegating the new one to buy the beer), the new young one might object to this practice. As the constitutive background of these subjects, everyday communication proceeds unproblematically, but as the story shows, there are times when what is taken for granted can be challenged: the young worker does not understand the linguistic meaning of the older worker's command or questions the factual information (there are no pubs selling beer nearby) or questions the appropriateness (what right does the older one have to order him) or questions the intentions of the older worker (is he trying to humiliate them?). When this occurs, there is a breakdown in the relationship between the speaker and the hearer, but in this case, it is not merely a breakdown of the linguistic-communicative competences, but of specific norms that are assumed within the lifeworld.

Linguistic communication proves crucial: it is because the experiences and situations that play out in the lifeworld are linguistically mediated that any breakdown in communications can be resolved. And once resolved, the lifeworld is transformed into a new space of shared meanings characterized by mutual understanding. When norms are challenged, repairing the breakdown in mutual understanding is possible because the lifeworld has within it the resources that enable the resolution of any challenges and a return to everyday intersubjective communication. However, Habermas points out that when this happens, only a particular feature or assumption is being challenged and not the lifeworld as a whole: 'Single elements, specific taken-granteds, are, however, mobilised in the form of consensual and yet problematisable knowledge only when they become relevant to a situation' (1987: 124).

One of Habermas's key concerns in his analysis of contemporary society is the threat posed to the lifeworld by the system. The system is typical of modern advanced mass societies whose large populations require that features of life that were coordinated within the lifeworld be transferred to self-regulatory systems whereby actions are controlled in an almost autonomous fashion. The lifeworld-system distinction is important because it allows Habermas to explain the way instrumental reasoning has infiltrated into the lifeworld, resulting in what he calls the 'colonization of the lifeworld' (1987: 355). Through the use of the non-linguistic 'steering media' of money and power, the system – by operating through the economy with instrumental action directed towards profit and the state with instrumental action directed at the administration of power – has taken a life of its own, corroding the sphere of the lifeworld. There are two key differences between the lifeworld and the system: the first is that the latter is parasitic upon the former. For the system to work, it must rely on the network of meaning that is generated within the lifeworld; secondly, while communicative action within the lifeworld entails understanding the reasons for achieving an action, the system does not require any knowledge of the reasons; it is only interested in the results. While the lifeworld is the social world with intersubjective communication directed at coordinating actions within society through mutual understanding, in the case of the system, the steering media of power and money take over intersubjective relations, eradicating the possibility of engaging communicatively with others to achieve understanding. The importance of the lifeworld for Habermas is that it enables him to find a balance between the rule-oriented formalism of universal pragmatics and the proceduralism of discourse ethics with an account that takes into consideration the particular contents of the lifeworld.

While the role of the lifeworld as a shared world needs to be presupposed in order to claim that intersubjective relations are always already constituted prior to the subject, it has been pointed out that Habermas's critique of the subject consists in establishing only a multiplication of subjects rather than providing an account of intersubjective relations (Young 1989: 213–25).

Conclusion

Both Schutz and Habermas constitute key points of reference for the rejection of the solitary or solipsistic subject by inverting the priority of the individual and the social. For both, the individual is always already situated within a world shared with Others with communicative interaction, both consolidating and enabling society to develop into more sophisticated forms of living together. For Schutz, the everyday world is intersubjective through and through and relations with Others are confirmed through communicative interactions, notably through the use of shared signs and symbols. For Habermas, the critique of the philosophy of the subject consists of the claim that communicative interaction presupposes intersubjective relations. In turn, communicative interaction creates a social reality with both social interaction and social integration functioning as constitutive elements of society insofar as they explain the way subjects relate to each other to coordinate actions as well as situating them within their lifeworld.

SECTION B

COMMUNICATION AND COMMUNITY

Since the revival of the debate on community in the 1980s, contemporary politics frequently invokes the concept of community, at times from opposing sides of the political spectrum. Orthodox Marxist accounts discussed the question of community reductively by focusing on its economic basis, whereas more recent debates have shifted the focus of the debate on the question of community and identity.

This debate has pitted communitarians (Anderson, MacIntyre, and Taylor) against libertarians. On the one hand, the communitarians emphasize the value of the community as a space of social bonding, a space that is organized around a common identity, and on the other hand, the libertarians emphasize the rights of the individual as over and above any social bonds. This debate had become somewhat stagnant but has since been revitalized with the intervention of Jean-Luc Nancy, who challenges the presuppositions of both communitarians and libertarians and, by so doing, provides a re-thinking of the question of community.

This chapter will examine the concept of community as it has been articulated by those who consider communication and the construction of a shared identity as a cohesive force for the community and those who consider communication as the key to creating communities with no shared identity. The central question that frames the debate on the formation of the community is this: on what grounds can one claim to be part of, or belong to a community? It is a crucial question, for questions of belonging are inevitably linked to questions of identification, to the way one identifies with a community. The logic operating behind this thinking of identity is one of inclusion and exclusion. The included are those who belong within a community; the excluded Others are those who do not but who – interestingly – make the limits of the community and who, paradoxically, are also necessary for the community that excludes them.

4

Mead and Carey on Community as 'Participation'

Introduction

George Herbert Mead and James Carey examine the question of community from the perspective of a shared identity constructed through the communicative efforts of the members of that community. Mead is chiefly remembered for his theory of symbolic interaction as well as his contribution to American pragmatism, and his ideas have been recognized by many, most notably by Habermas. The key to his account of community is the concept of 'co-operation', and in this respect, it is communication that enables and enhances the organization of the community as a 'generalized Other'. For Carey, influenced by Dewey's understanding of the dynamics of communication and community, an analysis of community needs to be integrated with an analysis of the processes of communication, and, in this respect, his shift away from the methods that emulated the natural sciences to his ritual or cultural model of communication proved fundamental.

In this chapter, I will elaborate on Mead's analysis of the nature of communication with the distinction he introduces to show the transition and continuity of non-verbal ('conversation of gestures') to verbal ('significant symbols') communication; following this, I will show how, on his account, linguistic communication enables the formation of the self as it interacts with Others and finally that this social interaction is transformed into a community or a 'generalized Other'. With Carey, I will first show the influence of Dewey's theory of communication upon him and follow this with an account of the interconnection between community and communication, with communication framed as ritualistic participation; finally, I will show how his later re-assessment of rituals as a possible form of exclusion is justified.

Mead on the nature of communication

Communication – nonverbal or gestural and verbal or linguistic – is fundamental to how Mead articulates his account of the self and society. He discusses these ideas in *Mind, Self and Society* (1934), where he takes a biological and behavioural account of what it is to be human as his point of departure. He argues that the social is grounded in the biological imperatives (sex and hunger) of its members who, crucially, deploy their communicative resources as the basis for the formation of their relationships together (1934: 227–28). Given the biological and behavioural underpinnings of communication, Mead introduces the distinction between the 'conversation of gestures' and 'the significant symbol', i.e. language. Despite being distinct, they are not opposed but instead form a continuum with the naturalism of the gesture supplemented with the notion of significance.

There are two important considerations to be made about the instinctive non-significant language of gestures and the significant language of symbols:

(a) the former is on a lower scale of animal evolution; it is also the means animals use for communication. The conversation of gestures is an instinctive form of communication characterized by a response to a stimulus that, in turn, generates a reaction and modification of behaviour. To illustrate his point, Mead uses the example of two dogs reacting to each other's movement – gestures – by changing their behaviour: the second dog retreats or attacks – responds – to the first dog – the stimulus. Their behaviour is meaningful, with the dogs communicating by virtue of their responses to each other. But while the dogs are conscious of each other, this form of communication does not entail self-consciousness because they act and react without knowing what they are doing. This is why, Morris elaborates, their communication cannot be considered a language: '[t]he meanings are not yet in mind, the biological individuals are not yet consciously communicating selves' (1934: XXI).

(b) in the case of the latter, while gestural communication entails no understanding by the entity of its gestures, with the use of significant symbols, we enter the domain of human action, which entails anticipating and understanding the meaning of the Other's intention and responding to it. This is the domain of self-consciousness: an animal is conscious of an external stimulus but not conscious of its response since it is instinctive. As humans are conscious of their responses, there is a qualitative and transformative change in their communication. By responding to the gesture in the same way as the Other does, by anticipating the response of the Other and acting accordingly, the gesture is now a significant symbol. 'Gestures become significant symbols when they implicitly arouse in an individual, making them the same responses

> which they explicitly arouse, or are supposed to arouse, in other individuals, the individuals to whom they are addressed' (1934: 47). Significant symbols are in effect linguistic, and this entails a shared meaning between speaker and hearer on account of the consciousness of their common response: '[w]here the gesture reaches that situation, it has become what we call "language." It is now a significant symbol, and it signifies a certain meaning' (1934: 46).

The distinction between gestures and symbols helps to elaborate Mead's account of meaning. 'Nature has meaning and implication but not indication by symbols. The symbol is distinguishable from the meaning it refers to. Meanings are in nature, but symbols are the heritage of man' (1934: 78). The key point is that meaning is relational in that it is the product of a response to a stimulus. On this account, the 'conversation of gestures' is also meaningful even though there is no accompanying consciousness: 'The mechanism of meaning is present in the social act before the emergence of consciousness or awareness of meaning occurs' (1934: 77). But while the context of relations has a meaning in itself, this meaning is not significant. It becomes significant when there is a self-conscious awareness of the response to the stimulus. This is important because the meaning of significant symbols is a common one, taking the form primarily of linguistic communication:

> The significant symbols is then the gesture, the sign, the word, which is addressed to the self when it is addressed to another individual, and is addressed to another, in form to all other individuals, when it is addressed to the self.
>
> (Mead 1922: 162)

The consequence of Mead's account of meaning is that given the interplay of symbols, responses, and subsequent actions, there can be no question that meaning is located in a person's solitary or private consciousness.

The question that becomes an issue for Mead is that of explaining how the gesture gets interpreted meaningfully by the Other. He dismisses the concept of imitation because imitation presupposes an identity of the stimulus with the response, an identity that is impossible to achieve (1934: 360–70). Mead proposes a behaviouristic explanation of meaning that centralizes the act as a response to a stimulus:

> They are acts which go beyond the organism taken by itself, but they belong to co-operative processes in which groups of animals act together, and they are the fulfilment of the processes which are essential to the life of the forms.
>
> (1934: 60)

The emergence of language as 'significant symbols' occurs when gestures become vocal, and it is here that the transformation from the animal to the human is enacted.

> What is peculiar to the latter is that the individual responds to his own stimulus in the same way as other people respond. Then the stimulus becomes significant; then one is saying something. As far as a parrot is concerned, its 'speech' means nothing, but where one significantly says something with his own vocal process he is saying it to himself as well as to everybody else within reach of his voice. It is only the vocal gesture to which one responds or tends to respond as another person tends to respond to it.
>
> (1934: 67)

The uniqueness of speech lies in the fact that, in the case of humans, the speaker is also their own listener. The speaker responds to the meaning of the utterance in the same way as other listeners respond to it. This is the 'double response' that Mead is alluding to, though why it should be the 'prototype' of all forms of communication is debatable (Tejera 1988: 53). The importance of the symbolic forms of communication is paralleled in Mead's celebrated account of role-playing. By adopting the role of the other person, the self can place itself in the position of the Other, which means that the self can understand the reaction of the Other in a given situation. It is because all participants respond in the same way to the speech that there is a shared meaning, allowing for co-operation between them.

This evolutionary development has had far-reaching consequences: human existence has been qualitatively transformed with the acquisition of speech because verbal communication makes more complex forms of human cooperation possible. For humans to interact co-operatively to develop more sophisticated societies, they must have been able to use language instrumentally to understand the meaning of actions and react accordingly.

Communication, minds and selves

Mead's analysis of the role of significant symbols introduces a further distinction between Minds and Selves. Gestures become significant symbols when there is a shared understanding of their response: Mead gives the example of a person shouting 'Fire' in a theatre. Just by shouting 'Fire!' the vocal gesture would not be significant, but it becomes significant because the speaker responds to the shout in the same way as the rest of the audience does. The mind or consciousness emerges when there is a common or 'significant' reaction to a situation so that the acquisition of language goes hand in hand with the emergence of the mind:

> Only in terms of gestures as significant symbols is the existence of mind or intelligence possible; for only in terms of gestures which are significant symbols can thinking – which is simply an internalised or implicit conversation of the individual with himself by means of such gestures – take place.
>
> (1934: 47)

The question of how the Self has emerged from the Mind is, for Mead, tied to two key features: (a) the evolutionary processes that brought about the development of certain physiological features, namely a complex central nervous system, vocalization as well as the use of the hand that enabled humans to control and analyse things, for humans; and (b) the social context wherein communicative interaction between the self and Others takes place (1934: 235). For Mead, the self does not emerge in a vacuum but only in relation to, and only after, its interaction with Others. The Other is the necessary condition for the emergence of the self because the Other makes it possible for the self to experience itself as an object. It is Others that enable the self to see itself as an object, and this is why, for Mead, the self knows itself indirectly, 'as he first becomes an object to himself just as other individuals are objects to him or in his experience; and he becomes an object to himself only by taking the attitudes of other individuals toward himself' (1934: 138). Against the view of the primacy of the self as an autonomous being, Mead highlights social relations: 'It is impossible to conceive of a self-arising outside of social experience' (1934: 140). By taking on the role of the Other, the individual is transformed into an object, and this, in turn, enables the self to emerge. This process can be observed in the development of children: when children play by taking on different roles, they create a self of themselves in relation to the Other. This is the beginning of the recognition of mutual and social relations. And it is by playing at being someone else that it realizes that it has a self that is different from that of others.

The role of communication in establishing how the self can be both an object and subject is highlighted by Mead:

> The importance of what we term 'communication' lies in the fact that it provides a form of behaviour in which the organism or the individual may become an object to himself [...] communication in the sense of significant symbols, communication which is directed not only to others but also to the individual himself.
>
> (1934: 138–39)

This is unique to humans insofar as the person can be both the subject and the object of their thoughts at the same time. Communication always presupposes and prioritizes the Other, and only after that does the sense of self emerge. While symbolic communication enables the emergence of the mind by way of response and readjustment to stimuli, the emergence of the self results from the objectivation of the self by the Other.

Communication and community

The importance of communication for the formation of the Self indirectly highlights the centrality of the community in Mead's social philosophy, for it is only within the community that the self arises, given that the individual both adopts the attitudes of Others and responds to those attributes itself. Self-consciousness is precisely this experience of becoming aware of the responses within oneself as they are experienced by Others.

Mead's analysis of the self is broadened to include all those Others that form a community into what he calls the 'generalized Other' as the ensemble of expectations, values and norms of Others. The 'generalized Other' contributes to the formation of the self as a social being by internalizing the expectations, values and norms of the Others within the community. Living in a community entails being able to see things from the perspective of others and putting oneself in the position of the Other; it entails a similarity of responses. This is a common feature of human behaviour, and it is important because by putting oneself in the place of the Other, one would respond to an experience or situation in the same way as the Other would.

> The significant gesture or symbols always presupposes for its significance the social process of experience and behaviour in which is arises; or, as the logicians say, a universe of discourse is always implied as the context in terms of which, or as the field within which, significant gestures of symbols do in fact have significance. This universe of discourse is constituted by a group of individuals carrying on and participating in a common social process of experience and behaviour, within which these gestures or symbols have the same or common meanings for all members of that group, whether they make them or address them to other individuals, or whether they overtly respond to them as made or addressed to them by other individuals.
> (1934: 89)

Given that Mead's thinking on the community is framed as co-operative activity, verbal communication becomes indispensable for the emergence of human communities. He is aware that insects and animals also display a remarkable degree of co-operation, so the question is to discover what differentiates them from human social activity. The answer he provides is naturalistic: in the case of insects, co-operation is determined by their physiology and the various functions that their species-specific physiological structures permit. And because their physiology does not permit variations, it is clear as to why co-operative activities within the insect world are always the same. With animals, it would seem that their behaviour involves more co-operation, but once again, their co-operation is entirely instinctive. For Mead, the crucial difference between animals and humans is that animals have not evolved a language of 'significant symbols', which is the necessary condition for human social organization; only humans have evolved an advanced central nervous system working in tandem with the vocal structures to produce linguistic communication. There can only be an organized human community when members of that community use language as a means of co-operation: '[i]n man the functional differentiation through language gives an entirely different principle of organisation which produces not only a different type of individual but also a different type of society' (1936: 244).

The distinction between the 'conversation of gestures' and 'significant symbols' once again comes into play, for while the former might be instinctive or automated, and therefore not require that the actions performed are understood by the participants (for e.g. bees in the construction of the bee-hive), in the case of significant symbols, communication is possible because in order to understand the meaning of vocal gestures, there must be a similarity of response by the Other and the self. 'It is out of this capacity for being influenced by our own gesture as we influence others that has arisen the peculiar form of the human social organism' (Mead 1934: 235).

Given that the emergence of sophisticated communities requires a complex system of communication, the further question concerns the way a community – as a shared world of expectations, values and norms – retains its identity over time. Mead explains this with the distinction between the I and the Me. This is important because while both are constitutive parts of the self, this distinction provides an explanation of the broader question of how change and stability within a society occur. The Me is the empirical, objective part of the self consisting of the internalized attitudes, roles and values of the community that the self internalizes as a member of that community: 'the "me" is the organised set of attitudes of others which one himself assumes' (1934: 175). Linguistic communication ensures the transmission of attitudes, roles and values to other members of the community, and in this way, the identity of the community is maintained and reproduced.

The I, on the other hand, 'is the response of the organism to the attitudes of the others' (1934: 175). It is the free, creative aspect of the self: it engages and challenges the values, attitudes and roles of the community. The Me represents the internalized norms of the community that exert pressure on the I so as to control it by establishing a limit on what is acceptable. There are parallels between the processes that take place on an individual level and on a broader social level. At an individual level, the 'I' is the personality that the self carves out for themself in relation to Others; here, it strives for uniqueness and difference. At a social level, the I is not just the internalization of the values, roles and attitudes of the community but also that which challenges the social order in the hope of transforming it. But while the I and the Me are analytically opposed, they are mutually interdependent. Just as there can be no I without a Me, there can be no Me without an I. And while the Me is the empirical self, the I is a kind of transcendental self that responds to and engages the Other:

> But what that a response will be he does not know and nobody else knows. Perhaps he will make a brilliant play or an error. The response to that situation as it appears in his immediate experience is uncertain, and it is that which constitutes the 'I'.
> (Mead 1934: 175)

The Me-I distinction accounts for change and stability within the community. It might seem that if the foundation of the community is what is common, then this might lead one to conclude that a community is 'destined' always to remain the same. But by introducing the I, Mead allows for the individual to bring specific experiences to the community, and these might bring about some change within it. A community is constituted, on the one hand, by the interplay of what is common to all, by what is taken for granted and accepted, and, on the other hand, by what is unique to the individual through the challenges and creativity brought by the individual. One can, by analogy, explain linguistic changes and innovation as the product of the interaction between 'sedimented forms' and 'novel forms' of linguistic usages that eventually became accepted by all.

Carey: the background: Dewey's theory of communication

Carey's innovative thinking about communication and mass communication stems from the backlash against the methodologies of the social sciences in the 1960s that attempted to mirror those used in the natural sciences. By using specific methodologies, the natural sciences explicitly assumed that their adherence would eventually – in progressive and linear steps – be able to provide an explanation of reality. But, just as these assumptions in the natural sciences were being challenged, likewise, the approaches towards the social sciences were judged as too reductive and ignorant of their political underpinnings.

A number of Carey's publications have been compiled into *Communication as Culture: Essays on Media and Society* (2008), and the ideas from the paper 'A cultural approach of communication' (1975) are central to this chapter. What the essays in this text and others show is the vast array of influences upon Carey's thought, ranging from Innis, Geertz, Weber, and Durkheim to Williams and Hoggart. But in relation to his writings on communication and community, it is perhaps Dewey who provides the basic framework for Carey, given that it was Dewey who first articulated the models of transmission and ritual as a way of explaining communication. Despite this influence, Carey was of the view that Dewey had failed to realize the problems inherent to these contrasting models and this, in turn, stimulated his 'larger project – the institution of the cultural approach to communication as a dominating paradigm of the field' (Sella 2007: 104).

The point of departure for understanding Dewey's concept of community and communication are the twin concepts of empathy and foresight. His analysis is speculative insofar as he seeks to understand the community by identifying the original moment whereby the animal was transformed into the human. That humans have existed together is not, for Dewey, something undeniable, but what is important is the way this being-together has been marked qualitatively by the emergence of 'intellectual properties'. This emergence mirrors the emergence of language, the latter also explained by reference to its origins in the natural world, where we find animals using signals to communicate. But signals are 'only' a proto-language and not a fully-fledged one since they lack a number of crucial features that can account for the emergence of language and community. With linguistic communication, signals are transformed into symbols when a common sphere of meaning is created that enables co-operative interaction.

> The heart of language is not 'expression' of something antecedent, much less expression of antecedent thought. It is communication, the establishment of cooperation in an activity in which there are partners, and in which the activity of each is modified and regulated by the partnership.
>
> (1929: 179)

Dewey's account of language depicts it as making possible other key features of human existence; his account is functional in that it is language that enables both foresight and empathy. With the emergence of symbols, it became possible to consciously use them so as to achieve complex patterns of thought that can be shared with others. Foresight constitutes the ability to predict outcomes and anticipate the behaviour of others. It is closely linked to empathy in that since one can anticipate the behaviour of the Other, then it would be possible to understand the situation they are in. As Belman points out, for Dewey both foresight and empathy can explain the social aspect of human existence as a co-operative one, and it is language that enables cooperative interaction (1977: 33).

The question that needs to be examined in Dewey's account is, therefore, that of the relation between symbols and thought. There are three 'discursive paths' (Belman 1977: 29–37) that explain this relation. These are

(a) the consensual aspect of symbols where a symbol acquires a meaning by virtue of the agreement on that symbol's use:

> A sound or mark of any physical existence is a part of *language* only in virtue of its *operational* force; that is, as it functions as a means of evoking different activities performed by different persons so as to produce consequences that are shared by all the participants in the conjoint undertaking.
>
> (Dewey 1938: 48, original emphasis)

(b) the nature of meaning that Dewey defines as 'rules for using and interpreting things, interpretation being always an imputation of potentiality for some consequence' (1929: 188). On his account, the meaning of something – whether symbolic or not – is tied to its effects on other persons or things. Symbolic communication attributes meanings to things by virtue of their use, and this, in turn, opens up the space for the possibility of different outcomes that foresight enables one to anticipate;

(c) the value of 'ideal experimentation': by this, Dewey points to the infinite creativity of language and foresight. The symbol, as Derrida points out, is not bounded by its context, thus allowing for the production of higher levels of sophistication:

> Events when once they are named lead an independent and double life. In addition to their original existence, they are subject to ideal experimentation: their meanings may be indefinitely combined and rearranged in imagination, and the outcome of this inner experimentation – which is thought – may issue forth in interaction with crude or raw events [...] Where communication exists, things in acquiring meaning thereby acquire representatives, surrogates, signs and implicates, which are infinitely more amenable to management, more permanent and more accommodating. then events in their first estate.
>
> (Dewey 1929: 166–67)

By using language in this way, it is possible to anticipate future possibilities and, therefore, adjust one's behaviour in light of these possibilities. It is the 'superiority' of language that enables humans to organize their social life as well as their intervention in the natural world.

It is clear that there is a continuum from language to the community. Dewey's account is naturalistic insofar as it explains the shift of prehistoric humans as biological animals living naturally and using signals as a form of communication to the human mode of existing by using symbols to communicate. This development, in turn, accelerated the development and complexity of the community as a world characterized by co-operation, empathy and foresight. But there is more to Dewey's speculations on the origins of the community: as a co-operative form of social existence, it contained within it the seeds for the evolution of a more complex community. His argument is that by identifying the origins of the community, he would be able to identify the ideal type of community, and this kind of community is possible only for and by humans because they have attained symbolic or linguistic communication.

In his articulation of the concept of community, Dewey was inspired by the early communities of the nineteenth century, for it was within these communities that he identified those features that would enable the revival of community in the twentieth century. Such a revival was needed because modernization generated a number of social problems that emerged with modernity's deviation from the ideals of these communities. A case in point is that of democratic participation, and Carey later adopted the idea of participation – as face-to-face conversation – in his elaboration of community and communication. But what is crucial for Carey's articulation is Dewey's re-thinking of communication and community:

> Society not only continues to exist *by* transmission, *by* communication, but it may fairly be said to exist *in* transmission, *in* communication. There is more than a verbal tie between the words common, community, and communication. Men live in a community in virtue of the things which they have in common; and communication is the way in which they come to possess things in common.
>
> (Dewey 2004: 4, original emphasis)

Here, the two transmission and ritual communication models are introduced and contrasted, providing the impetus for Carey's sustained and in-depth analysis.

Carey on the interrelation between communication and community

An analysis of the concept of the multiple forms of communication shows that it is so prevalent that it is taken for granted, in much the same ways as the air we breathe is taken for granted. Carey (2008) highlights this because its all-pervasiveness produces the result that the study of communication is not taken as seriously as it should be, even given that communication – from the ordinary to the sophisticated – is the foundation of human existence. Central to Carey's concept of communication is its all-encompassing organizing function: 'Communication is a symbolic process whereby reality is produced, maintained, repaired and transformed' (2008: 19). Communication enables humans to co-produce and share meaning: it brings social reality into being, maintains it, fixes it when it breaks down, and sometimes changes it. The question that needs answering concerns the way meaning is produced and, in opposition to the then prevalent view, Carey did not focus on the study of codes but on the way meaning was ritualized by participants in a community.

By way of showing the centrality of communication to human existence, Carey introduces the term 'map' to describe the way communication is both a representation 'of' reality as well as a guide 'for' reality. Communication plays a twofold role in human existence: it entails both a descriptive and normative element, telling us what the world is like and how to live in it. Given that different societies have different systems of communication, the implication is that they experience different realities: 'To live within the purview of different maps is to live within different realities' (2008: 22). This distinction is useful insofar as it reveals that the meanings inherent to human communication are not just descriptive but that these can, in turn, be questioned. What Carey is presenting is an account of communication that is both dynamic and reflective because a fundamental aspect of human existence is that humans think about the meanings that guide their lives.

In order to understand the way the concept of communication has been tied historically to the formation of community, Carey takes as his point of departure the appearance of the terminology of 'communication' within American culture in the twentieth century. His analysis reveals that (a) there were two models of communication being utilized simultaneously; (b) the modernization of American culture and communication emerged out of a religious context (2008: 13–14).

By identifying the way the concept of communication was used in the nineteenth century, Carey goes on to trace its permutation into the later narrower transmission model of communication that was hugely influential in the twentieth century. In its original context, the concept of communication was used in a twofold manner to explain both the transportation of material goods as well as the transportation of information or messages. The symmetry between both is understandable given that, at the time, messages and goods were transported together on trains and, therefore, travelled at the same speed. The invention of the telegraph changed this radically: the speed with which messages arrived at their destination outpaced that of goods, with the result that the terminology of communication was narrowed to the transmission of information. Its contemporary usage 'is also related strongly to the nineteenth-century desire to use communication and transportation to extend influence, control, and power over wider distances and over greater populations' (Carey 1977: 412).

The transmission model became the dominant model of communication across various disciplines in America in the twentieth century, in particular, with the way it was formulated by Shannon and Weaver and others as the linear or bullet model of communication. But the point Carey establishes through his genealogical analysis is that despite the twentieth-century aspirations to be secular and scientific, religious values and beliefs are presupposed by the transmission model. The underlying religious presupposition can be traced back to the arrival of Christian migrants in the United States who dreamt of a 'New Jerusalem' where the life of faith could be lived to the full, creating a paradise on earth. But as they travelled across the United States, they came into contact with the local pagan communities, and this encounter obliged them to re-think their mission so as also to spread the word of God and convert the local population. The technology of the telegraph was enlisted to further the Christian message insofar as it could now be transmitted across even greater distances and at greater speeds. The telegraph enabled control to be exerted over large distances, with the management of space becoming part of the apparatus of the transmission model.

While over time, the United States slowly shifted from a religious to a secular culture, the idea of control that was inherent to the transmission model was re-adapted for the attainment of ideological goals. Carey (2008: 109–32) identified a number of key features of the transmission model: it was a 'power' that would control and modify the behaviour of others across vast distances. It was instrumental and message-oriented, using strategies of persuasion to achieve this end with the markers of success identified as those that are most efficient in bringing about the desired results. Implicit in this model was a top-bottom hierarchy with those in control at the top, sending messages to the 'masses' at the bottom. To analyse the efficiency of the messages transmitted, what was required was an examination of the effects of those messages upon the audience, the receivers. This became known as the 'effects tradition' valorizing quantitative research that used a scientific methodology.

The other model that Carey identifies within American culture is that of ritual; it is the counterpart to the transmission model, existing prior to it and emphasizing the communal aspect of communication. The ritual model 'of communication is not directed toward the extension of messages in space, but the maintenance of society in time; not the act of imparting information or influence but the creation, representation, and celebration of shared beliefs' (1977: 412). The articulation and terminology of rituals that Carey adopted from Durkheim bring out the 'participatory' and 'sharing' aspects of community, of communion with others.

While it might seem that rituals belong to some 'earlier' premodern type of society, social life in contemporary society is still infused with rituals: sports, political and religious events all induce a sense of participation and community. But everyday conversation is also ritualistic in the sense that it also structures and gives a sense of order to everyday reality. It is in this sense that Carey thinks of communication as ritualistic in that it brings people together and establishes social relations. The ritual model of communication is also important for framing the identity of the community because rituals make it possible for a community to continue to exist; the temporal dimension of rituals ensures the maintenance and reproduction of a community. Ritualistic communication is central here because it provides an intersection by bringing the past to the present and pointing towards the future.

However, Carey's emphasis on rituals did not extend to those rituals that entailed technologies of communication. His argument was that rituals, from everyday conversation to the more elaborate forms, are embodied activities requiring the co-presence of participants. Conversation entails 'activating and displaying all the capacities of the body' (1997: 314). The presence of the Other in face-to-face communication completes the conversation insofar as verbal and non-verbal cues or feedback are taken into consideration, allowing for the strengthening or the changing of views.

The dismissal of the ritualistic or cultural approaches to communication in U.S culture has occurred, according to Carey, for two reasons: (a) the American overvaluation of the individual, the psychological life and the idea that the good life is one of productivity; (b) the false dichotomy between science and culture, with science as the delivery of objectivity truth and culture as the space of subjectivity and error. This dichotomy was problematic insofar as it promoted the view that only science constituted what counted as knowledge and, furthermore, that the methods of the natural sciences should be used to study society (Subtil 2014: 19–24).

There has been considerable debate as to whether the transmission-ritual distinction is a rigid one, with each term excluding the other (Cmiel 1992: 285–290), or whether there is some overlap between them. While it is clear that there are very specific differences between them, I would suggest that Carey *avant* Derrida deconstructs the transmission-ritual opposition by inverting the hierarchy that privileged transmission with that of ritual and generalizing the concept of ritual to include with it the concept of transmission. It should be remembered that Carey's valorization of the ritual model was intended as a counterweight to the then dominance of the transmission model that had neglected the binding force of communication. Carey, too, recognized the limitation of adopting a mutually exclusive opposition of both models:

> A ritual view does not exclude the processes of information transmission or attitude change. It merely contends that one cannot understand these processes aright

> except insofar as they are cast within an essentially ritualist view of communication and social order.
>
> (2008: 17)

The recognition of this can be seen in his analysis of newspapers from both perspectives. In the case of the transmission model, a newspaper would be considered a source of information for the public insofar as this information is transmitted throughout the country, and its analysis would entail examining the effects of this information on the public. With the ritual model, the analysis would focus on the way the audience participated in the news, engaging in dialogical interaction and, by so doing, creating a shared reality. But, to be clear, the 'sharing of reality' does not mean that among the audience, there is a consensus on what this reality in question is; on the contrary, even if it is shared, the meaning of events or situations can become sites of contestation.

Answering the question of the relationship between the community and communication was important insofar as it enabled Carey to provide an answer to: 'the problem of how persons and societies work when they are working effectively' (2008: 69). This was, and still remains, one of the central questions of social theory: how is social order possible given the different individuals with their individual and conflicting desires?

The power of rituals

One of the persistent questions that scholars bring up concerns the extent of Carey's neglect of the role of power in the dynamics of the community. It has been claimed that his position on communication as ritual neglects the forces of power and conflict that have characterized human societies and, in particular, the seeming resistance to change that ritual implies. Such a characterization of society would find adherents within the Marxist tradition that centralized exploitation as the way to understanding social relations. Despite being sympathetic to the left, Carey did not think that the Marxist understanding of power in terms of a centralized power structure and the conflict between classes was the key to understanding society. In addition, Carey also disagreed with Marxist reductive explanations of society by discovering 'laws' – and in this case, economic ones – that would explain all social processes. Rather, Carey's analysis was informed by the liberal tradition and, in the same spirit as Dewey, he focused on the way the notion of community can be retrieved and deployed in a contemporary context.

But the association of community with the liberal tradition and democracy creates other problems: (a) by neglecting to take into consideration the dynamics of power in contemporary society, this indirectly left the space for the neo-liberal valorization of the market, and, if unregulated opened the door to those forces that destroy community, that he was to retrieve; (b) by focusing on the way the community co-creates and shares symbols Carey's analysis is lopsided because it does not factor in the power involved in the creation of these symbols. It is often the case that those with more power have more say in the production of symbols (Ross 2013).

In Carey's defence, while his focus on interpersonal relations did not entail taking power dynamics into consideration, he conceded that with mass communication, 'questions of political power and institutional change are inescapable' (2008: 53). What becomes increasingly evident to Carey is that power is not opposed to ritual because power has its own rituals, with conflict and opposition becoming ritualized. And while rituals are forms of participation and belonging, they can also become – as sites of contestation over meanings – forms of exclusion.

In 'Political ritual on television: Episodes in the history of shame, degradation and excommunication', Carey (1998: 42–70) discusses the unsuccessful hearing of Judge R. H. Bork for confirmation before the Senate. This was a case of a ritual performed within a democratic system before the authorities who had the power to exclude those who held different systems of belief, with Bork, in this case, considered an outsider to mainstream US systems of belief. To highlight this abuse of rituals, Carey introduces the terminology of 'excommunication' with the tension at the heart of rituals, being that their (positive) binding power comes about by virtue of their (negative) exclusion of others. For Sella (2007: 117), Carey's mistake is that of generalizing from this specific case into a broader indictment of ritualized events within American culture, despite the fact that this instance of ritualized excommunication did not undermine the American system at all. The deeper problem, for Sella, is that once the authority of a ritual of excommunication is established, there is no way of

> telling how the forces that control it and direct it would play out, and who would be their chosen subject of exclusion. They bear a risk of systematic cruelty not from the kind that forestalls a promotion, but the kind that disenfranchises and derogates minorities, and acts out institutionalised racism.
>
> (2007: 118)

Sella suggests that to counter the threat of ritualized exclusionary politics, what is needed is a reconfiguration of ritual communication to include the transmission mode of communication on the grounds that its methodology can be used to identify the strategies of persuasion within ritualized communication deployed by those in power. To support this suggestion, Sella provides three scenarios (2007:

121–23) where the transmission model (a) can reveal the extent of the effectiveness of persuasion in ritual communication, (b) can show how effective rituals themselves are and (c) can be used to see if ritual communication has consolidated or disrupted core community values.

Conclusion

Both Mead and Carey consider the concept of communication as pivotal in the formation of a community. For Mead, this entails providing an account that is grounded in biology so as to provide an explanation of the way communication emerges out of a natural environment in which the social precedes the individual, with the social dimension of communication as key to constituting a community. For Carey, inspired by Dewey's theory of communication, the formation of community through communication requires a recuperation of the concept of ritual insofar as rituals bring people together to participate in a shared identity. To this effect, he positions himself in opposition to the transmission model of communication that treats subjects as abstractions from their community. Over time, however, he came to realize that the power attributed to rituals might itself fracture the identity of the community that they were supposed to bring about.

5

Agamben on Community as 'Communicability'

Introduction

Agamben's interest in language and communication is evident in several writings. This interest is tied to his view of the communicativity of language as communication that enables the re-thinking of the political and the ethical. Although commentators have chiefly focused on the latter aspects of this work, language and communication play a critical theoretical role in his analysis of the concept of community. And while their role in *The Coming Community* (1993) has been acknowledged and commented upon, their centralizing role has perhaps been understated. What Agamben proposes in this text is a new model for living together that challenges the concept of belonging itself insofar as it differentiates people into an 'us and them' dialectic. Agamben's strategy for his communal vision is to overcome this dialectical opposition by 'freezing' the terms in the opposition such that they are rendered, to use his terminology 'inoperative'.

In this chapter, I will highlight the crucial role that the writings of Walter Benjamin and Guy Debord play upon Agamben in his articulation of the coming community; following this, I will elaborate on the nature of the community that he calls 'pure singularities' that will in turn lead to an examination of communication in contemporary 'spectacular' society. In the final section, I will examine Agamben's introduction of the concept of communicability in the coming community.

The influence of Benjamin and Debord on the coming community

Both W. Benjamin and G. Debord play crucial formative roles in Agamben's philosophy, and their ideas are particularly evident in *The Coming Community*. In this section, I will provide an overview of their ideas as they contribute specifically to Agamben's articulation of the community.

In 'On language as such and on the language of man' (2002: 62–74), Benjamin distinguishes between the language of man and language in general. The latter is broader and includes the former, but for Benjamin, it is the language of man as a language that names that provides the key to understanding the nature of language. In his account of language, Benjamin connects language as naming to human existence, arguing against any abstract theory of language that separates them because this would ignore what is crucial about human existence, namely, that by naming, humans communicate their existence.

In this respect, Benjamin also writes that human language is an expression of a 'mental entity'. This might be misleading if one puts mental states on one side and language on the other. It is not what Benjamin thinks: instead, mental states can only be articulated in language; for him, there is no bifurcation of language and thought. What is innovative about this is that the medium of communication, language, and what is communicated, the word, are one and the same. This dual role of language constitutes a paradox that any theoretical account would typically attempt to resolve. For Benjamin, it is not a question of resolution but one of transformation so that the paradoxical nature of language is transformed into a theory that brings out what is unique about language, namely, the human production of names.

Naming is defined as 'that *through* which, and *in* which, language itself, and nothing more, communicates itself absolutely' (2002: 65, original emphasis). For Benjamin, language is itself only when it communicates linguistically, and in particular, in the act of naming. His account of the name counters the tendency to think of the language–world relationship as one where, on the one side, the world exists prior to and independent of language, and on the other, there is language that represents it. The difference between this representational account that makes language in a sense 'dependent' on the world and Benjamin's account can be seen in his own example of the word and the object 'lamp'. While the name 'lamp' and the object 'lamp' are obviously very different, the object can only be communicated about in language. Because language can only communicate how the lamp exists through the medium of language, Benjamin writes, 'Language communicates the linguistic being of things' (2002: 65).

In response to the possible objection that saying the name-lamp is communicated in language is merely a tautology, Benjamin responds that it is more than a tautology because language communicates both the name and the fact that it is communicating. These two features occur at the same time, at the moment when language is being used. What is striking is his emphasis on the communicability of language itself, independently of its content or of any speakers. Benjamin calls the dual aspect of language as the medium of communication and what is meant by communication the 'magic of language' (2002: 64).

As it turns out, the 'magic of language' is also its 'primary problem'. For Benjamin, language and mental existence are interrelated, such that you cannot have mental states without language. What he considers to be the problem of language is that it both mediates mental existence and, at the same time, is intertwined with mental existence. It cannot be the case that mental existence is communicated through language because this would make mental existence seem like objects or things in the world that are represented through language. But, the relation between mental existence and language is different from the relationship between language and the world: for Benjamin, mental existence communicates in (not through) language so that language performs the double feat of mediating a mental existence that is only immediately found in language.

The target of Benjamin's theory of language as representation is what he calls 'the bourgeois conception of language', a conception that reduces language to an instrumental and functional way of thinking. On the contrary, Benjamin thinks of language as unlimited: 'what is communicated *in* language cannot be externally limited or measured, and therefore all language contains its own incommensurable, uniquely constituted infinity. Its linguistic being, not its verbal contents, defines its frontier' (2002: 64, original emphasis). It is the infinity of language that is the enabling feature of its productivity: there are no limits to the freedom of language in the production of names. In his account of the magical aspect of language, Benjamin emphasized the perhaps underrated communicability of language itself. However, this is one pole of the equation: the other pole is the production of names, and with this, he also wants to acknowledge that the communicative act is also about something else that has been given a name. There are significant consequences to this: being named means objects or the natural world is transformed into the realm of knowledge. While, clearly, objects or the natural world do not have a language, humans name them and, with this act, make them knowable.

In his analysis of the name, Benjamin contrasts the human relation to names with the theological account of naming. In the theological account, the act of naming and creating are one and the same; when God names something, he brings it into existence. On the other hand, the human relation to names is different because, for humans, naming brings things within categories of knowledge. What this comparison shows is that the human relation is one of difference, with names being different from things, and by so doing, enabling knowledge to be acquired, while the relation of God to names is one of identity, with names as identical to things.

The goal of Benjamin's digression into the theological account of naming is not to dismiss theology but to express a broader and overarching vision of language as an 'ultimate reality' (2002: 67). By this, he means that language is the beginning and the end of everything and this is what language as a medium of communication, communicates, enabling humans to achieve knowledge of the world for it is because humans are aware of language as naming that they can differentiate between names and things.

The second key influence on Agamben is Guy Debord and the Situationist International. In *The Society of the Spectacle* (2002) Debord undertakes an analysis of the emerging society of the twentieth century, dominated by images:

> The spectacle is the stage at which the commodity has succeeded in totally colonizing social life. Commodification is not only visible, we no longer see anything else; the world we see is the world of the commodity. Modern economic production extends its dictatorship both extensible and intensively.
>
> (2002: 21)

The concept of the Spectacle they introduced was visionary and is now part of the lexicon of everyday life. But while common parlance thinks of the spectacle narrowly in terms of entertainment, the concept of the Spectacle that Debord introduced is totalizing in the sense that the Spectacle had taken over reality: 'The spectacle is the map of this new world, a map that is identical to the territory it represents' (2002: 16). As a result, what needed to be worked out were the implications for everyday social reality.

Debord presents several 'theses' that describe post-war capitalism and the consumer society associated with it; his basic argument is that a new type of society has emerged from the development of media and communication technologies. What Debord undertakes is an analysis of social reality as it was emerging in the aftermath of the Second World War, where American soldiers, returning home with money in their pockets, found a society that provided a vast range of consumer goods for them. By the 1950s, the consumer society was born in the United States, and by the 1960s, it had reached Europe. Given these developments, in his view, it was increasingly evident that capitalism was transitioning to a new stage of development from an economy focused on forms of production to one organized around consumption, the media and technology. The increasing use of media technologies from the 1930s (radio, photography) onwards to spread political propaganda and the use of celebrities to provide an alternative world for those mired in poverty set the stage for what Debord predicted would become the society of the spectacle.

The emergence of this new world of the spectacle called for a new kind of social analysis. While orthodox Marxist theory focused its analysis on the factory and class struggle, Debord broadened his analysis while still retaining Marxist insights into capitalism and commodification in everyday life, with culture playing a pivotal role in transforming society. Debord and the Situationist focus on everyday life was inspired by Lefebvre and Sartre's views on the concept of the situation that, for the latter, described the embeddedness of human existence, and for the former, the need to undertake revolutionary practice in everyday life. Debord and the Situationists adopted the concept of the situation to argue for the need to create new situations in everyday life.

The opening line of *The Society of the Spectacle* is both an appropriation and reconfiguration of Marx's introduction to Capital: 'In societies dominated by modern conditions of production, life is presented as an immense accumulation of *spectacles*. Everything that was directly lived has receded into a representation' (2002: 7, original emphasis). This citation points to the fact that while capitalism still operates by producing commodities, this production has been abstracted to an even higher level, where the spectacle of the commodity is prioritized and given value. The success of the Spectacle is that the world of objects is transformed into a world of images. The value of objects is now reconstructed by capitalism as not merely a question of 'having' the object but one of how it appears, i.e. its value as an image (2002: 10–11).

But while the vast array of consumer goods coupled with images deployed to attract consumers ultimately led to a world dominated by the Spectacle, the critical point for understanding advanced capitalism is that it marked a shift in human relations: 'The Spectacle is not a collection of images; it is a social relation between people mediated by images' (2002: 7). The concept of 'spectacle' has enabled Debord to identify how capitalism has transformed subjects into spectators. They are spectators in the sense that they consume the world as it appears to them through images: it is the world of image-related goods as well as the images produced by the media industries. All these operations of capitalism are directed at producing docile subjects living in a 'permanent opium war' (2002: 22). In so doing, capitalism is able – without using violence – to manipulate and control subjects by creating their desires that can only be satisfied through consumption.

The world of the Spectacle is a world that encourages 'separation'. One of the dominant and insidious ways capitalist spectacles separate persons is through the many cultural forms proliferating social life: the leisure industry has become commodified, producing various forms of cultural entertainment, which in turn further separate persons from their lives. Each person is concerned now with the personal enjoyment that the leisure industries provide. This insight reveals the structural changes that Debord highlighted: whereas early capitalism defined the worker as a producer, with the structural change brought about by the Spectacle, the worker was defined as a consumer. The advantage of this new shift for capitalism is that, in contrast to early capitalism, it was always possible for workers to revolt against their exploitation; with the capitalism of the Spectacle, workers have been transformed into willing consumers who celebrate the spectacle that dominates them.

The separation of the Spectacle also operates internally as a form of self-alienation that distracts persons from living their lives to the full. Debord's thinking and critique of the world of images is structured along a contrast between representation and experience, between an indirect and a direct mode of existence. The Spectacular world is a world of representation that has taken over the world of lived experience:

> The more he contemplates, the less he lives; the more he identifies with the dominant images of need, the less he understands his own life and his own desires. The spectacle's estrangement from the acting subject is expressed by the fact that the individual's gestures are no longer his own; they are the gestures of someone else who represents them to him.
>
> (2002: 16)

Debord introduces a further qualification to the analysis of the Spectacle, presenting a difference between the Spectacle as 'concentrated' and 'diffused'. The 'concentrated' describes totalitarian and 'Stalinist' regimes that use force and the cult of personality to control subjects, and 'diffuse' describes capitalist–democratic systems that use a vast array of commodities coupled with the notion of the freedom to choose as a way of control by promoting the illusion that that subjects are themselves in control by choosing what to consume. Whereas the 'concentrated' spectacle is blatantly brutal, the 'diffuse' spectacle is insidious because it constantly creates and re-creates the desires for the commodities the subject thinks they are free to choose from. In his later text, *Comments on the Society of the Spectacle* (1988), Debord introduced a new term, the 'integrated' Spectacle, and this was a combination of the other two. His assessment of this new form of the Spectacle was bleak: 'there remains nothing, in culture or nature, which has not been transformed, and polluted according to the means and interests of modern industry' (1990: 10).

On the community of the 'pure singularity'

The point of departure for Agamben's critical engagement with the concept of community is that of challenging the concept of belonging, which functions as a key concept in delineating how a community is formed. The process of belonging operates through a logic of inclusion, the basis of which is a shared characteristic that enables a communal identity to be established. This is the philosophy of community espoused by communitarians such as MacIntyre, and which Agamben – together with others – rejects on the grounds that belonging and identity, by definition, exclude those who do not share in this identity. Agamben's critique is directed at disrupting the logic of inclusion and exclusion that is implied by the concept of belonging. In his vision, those who do not belong are those who do not fit into a community's self-identification and are therefore excluded: they include migrants, refugees' prisoners of concentration camps, and also patients and poets. The concept of community will be reclaimed, 'not for another class nor for the simple generic absence of any belonging, but for being-*such*, for belonging itself' (1993: 2, original emphasis).

The 'coming community' is the expression he uses to describe the community of subjects without communal markers of identity. These are the 'Whatever being' and: 'The Whatever in question here relates to singularity not in its indifference with respect to a common property (to a concept, for example: being red, being French, being Muslim), but only in its being *such as it is*' (1993: 1, original emphasis).

The phrase 'such as it is' acknowledges the value of the singular in that it 'always matters' that we recognize singularities independently of any markers of identity. The onus of this recognition lies with the 'Whatever' as it will bypass or undo the dialectical opposition between the singular and the universal or, as it can also be formulated, between the part and the whole. The relationship between these terms is fundamental in that the singular derives its meaning and identity by being subsumed within the universal or colloquially by the part being integrated into the whole. It is this dialectical opposition that has generated the problem of belonging since the way a singular is subsumed by the universal or the part integrated within the whole is determined by the logic of inclusion and exclusion.

This is an old problem in the tradition of philosophy, and as Agamben rightly points out, it is a problem that 'has its origins in language. The word "tree" designates all trees indifferently, insofar as it posits the proper universal significance in place of singular ineffable trees' (1993: 9). What is at stake is the transformation of the singular into the universal. When one talks about a concrete, specific singularity, 'this car', its singularity is transformed into a universal or a general term, 'car' in accordance with certain characteristics. The process that transforms the singular into a universal takes place through language, and the singular is lost to the universal. A similar occurs with the formation of political communities whereby single individuals become members of a community by sharing or holding something in common, even if they do not necessarily know or approve of the Others in the community. For both language and the formation of a political community, what is specific to the individual is 'lost' in this process of generalization. This is an unavoidable problem given that all language, of necessity, utilizes universal or general terms.

For Agamben, the quest for the singular is a quest to go beyond the predicates of identity since the singular is more than all the predicates combined. Agamben's strategy is to 'freeze' this opposition, and Watkin lucidly highlights this:

> Agamben does not seek to solve the problem of part and whole [...] but instead seeks to use the problem to step out of the debate altogether through the formulation of his conceptualisation of whatever singularities or the being as-such of beings [...] singularity is the very point of indifference between the unknowability of multiple particulars and the supersensuous reductive abstraction of general laws.
>
> (2014: 67)

On his account, the singular transmits a plenitude of being that is not reducible to categorization. In his example, the singularity of a loved one goes beyond any labelling: 'The lover wants the loved one *with all of its predicates*, its being such as it is' (1993: 2, original emphasis). The loved one is loved for the 'plenitude' of its being rather than a specific quality. To elaborate on the irreducibility of the singular, Agamben draws an analogy between the singularity of the word and the singularity of the face. What the analogy serves to show is that in the case of both, there is an 'inessential' relationship between the common and the singular:

> Just as the right human word is neither the appropriation of what is common (language) nor the communication of what is proper, so too the human face is neither the individuation of a generic *facies* nor the universalisation of singular traits: It is whatever face, in which what belongs to common nature and what is proper are absolutely indifferent.
>
> (1993: 19, original emphasis)

It could rightly be said that the whatever singular is also the whatever face. What this means is that just as there is no ideal or universal face that manifests itself in a specific face, and neither is there one specific face that represents all faces, the relationship between face – as a common feature of humans – and the specific face of the individual is 'absolutely indifferent'.

But, Agamben adds, although the relationship between the generic and the individual is 'inessential', the two terms 'interpenetrate'. This applies to both language and the face. The point is that no rigorous boundary can be specified in the movement from general to particular or particular to general. To describe this back-and-forth movement, Agamben adopts the metaphor of the line in opposition to some teleological goal that culminates with the whatever. He illustrates this interpenetration with an example from language: just as one cannot separate the letters of the alphabet (a general form) from the writing that identifies the individual, likewise, it is from one's individual handwriting (or pronunciation) that the alphabet as a formal system can be identified. In other words:

> The passage from potentiality to act, from language to the word, from the common to the proper, comes about every time as a shuttling in both directions alone a line of sparkling alternation on which common nature and singularity, potentiality and act change roles and interpenetrate. The being that is engendered on this line is whatever being. (1993: 20)

However, despite the seeming inescapability of the singular–universal dialectic, language provides a resource that makes it possible to think past this opposition. For Agamben, the 'example' provides the linguistic resource to move beyond this opposition: 'Neither particular nor universal, the example is a singular object that presents itself as such, that *shows* its singularity', adding that 'Exemplary Being is purely linguistic being' (1993: 10, original emphasis). The figure of the example operates to disrupt both inclusion and exclusion from the category of belonging: to say, 'There were many cruel people in history, such as, for example, Adolf Hitler' is a case of Hitler being a member of the class of 'cruel people'. But taken on his own, he does not constitute the entire class of cruel people and, in this sense, is excluded from it. The singularity of the example works because it straddles the logic of inclusion and exclusion. As De la Durantaye writes, 'Via the figure of the example, a nondialectical relation in which the singularity or example, is at once a member of, and excluded from, the set of things it exemplifies' (2009: 163).

The strategic value of the example for Agamben's view is that it offers an innovative way of thinking about the relationship of the singular to the universal, of the part to the whole. It freezes the dialectic with a new term that does not negate any of the other terms but proceeds by folding these terms into each other, a process of involution. As a result, he can justify a new communal formation as one whose membership is constituted by a 'form of non-identity'. The terminology of indifference in Agamben's earlier citation is positive: the singular is exemplary in that it is indifferent to the usual forms of belonging defined according to certain specific and necessary conditions. There will be no conditions for belonging in the 'coming community': it will be a community without an identity. As Agamben writes, 'These pure singularities communicate only in the empty space of the example, without being tied by any common property, by any identity' (1993: 11–12).

Communication in the spectacular society

In *The Coming Community*, Debord is a crucial formative influence in Agamben's thinking on the political dimension of the 'coming community'. Debord's analysis of the 'society of the spectacle' exposed the domination of society through the circulation of the image following the dictates of capital, concluding that contemporary spectacular society is totalizing in the sense that (a) it is so pervasive level that there is no space in social life that is unaffected by the images that circulate within it; (b) it provides us with the illusion of freedom and choice, and yet, next to nothing can be done to change it. In sum, the society of the spectacle is overwhelming and complete.

Agamben recognizes the insightfulness of Debord's analysis of contemporary capitalism, which shows how the alienation and exploitation of others take place through the 'spectacle'. But he adds an interesting twist to Debord's analysis of the spectacle with the claim that 'the spectacle is language, the very communicativity or linguistic beings of humans' (1993: 80). So while for Debord, the spectacle has alienated humans through the proliferation and circulation of images in everyday life, Agamben considers the spectacle to be 'the alienation of language itself, of the very linguistic and communicative nature of humans' (1993: 80). This stage of spectacular capitalism constitutes a serious development in that it is the linguistic being of humans, their 'essence' that has been appropriated. It is not just that the spectacle has normalized consumption and the patterns of alienation that go with it but has alienated humans from their essential being. Spectacular capitalism has appropriated communication for its own purposes, as a means of separation, exploitation and alienation, in contrast to communication that is used to connect with others. It has taken away the 'communion' from communication, a predicament that De La Durantaye clearly describes: 'The spectacle reaches not only into our homes through the ideological messages transmitted by our media but also our very "mediality" – our capacity to communicate what we have in common' (2009: 174).

By elaborating on what he has in mind with the concept of communicative alienation, Agamben provides an interpretation of the story of the Shekinah from the Hebrew tradition. For him, 'isolation of the Shekinah' is an instance of a type of communication that is no longer linked to the everyday life of humans but has become 'separated is an autonomous sphere' (1993: 80.1). According to Agamben, the figure of Aher is central insofar as his attempt at 'cutting off the branches' is an attempt at acquiring knowledge and obtaining mastery of just one aspect of the divine (1993: 80.1). By isolating and contemplating knowledge, Aher has, in effect, dislocated knowledge from its grounding in lived experience, and it is this dislocation that mirrors the communicative alienation of the spectacle: just as knowledge in Aher's world is a pseudo-knowledge, the reality of the spectacle is a pseudo-reality: in both cases, what is apparent is being mistaken for what is real, where non-communication is confused with real communication.

Agamben's analysis of contemporary alienation is extended to his reading of a 1970s advert on stockings called 'Dim'. While the advert depicted women dancing, it was created in such a way that it simultaneously produced both 'communication and estrangement'. Agamben points out that theorists had read this commodification of the human body as more than another instance of capitalist production, a new phenomenon that needed deciphering. The commodification of the body – its transformation into an exchange value – undermined the importance that biology and biography (the uniqueness of the individual) had contributed to creating the 'stigma of ineffability'. As a result, the body became 'for the first time perfectly communicable, entirely illuminated' (1993: 48). The processes of commodification, coupled with the technological innovations evidenced by the industries, displaced the value that theology had attributed to the body in the past. Given this displacement, Agamben re-assesses the 'liberated' body as having the potential of 'something truly whatever' because as a whatever body, it '*is a resemblance without archetype – in other words, an Idea*' (1993: 48). The body has become the site of possibilities not tied to any preconceived notions of identity.

In addition, given how the world of advertising and capitalist commodification has permeated all aspects of social life, the body has been divested of any value. It has done this through a process whereby the image and the body have been separated, with the image functioning as both a spectacle and as a 'mask' that hides the reality of bodies. As Agamben pointedly reminds us, these bodies die daily along the highways or have died in the death camps. It is only by overcoming this dualism of body and image that the space for the 'whatever body' will be carved out of the capitalist system, a system that focuses on the image at the expense of the body. The whatever body, as Agamben articulates it, is composed of both, and together, they constitute the whatever singularity, the singular body that has the possibility of creating its own image. The possibility of the emergence of the 'whatever singularity' and the escape from the intrusion and domination of the spectacle in everyday life is, ironically, tied to the world of advertising and pornography that has become 'the unknowing midwives of this new body of humanity' (1993: 50).

On Agamben's account, it would seem that the totalizing force of the spectacle, with its appropriation of the communicative essence of humans, has rendered any hope for resisting and changing it futile: 'What hampers communication is communicability itself, humans are separated by what unites them. Journalists and mediacrats are the new priests of this alienation from human linguistic nature' (1993: 83). Ironically, however, he suggests that the 'alienation from linguistic being' caused by the 'democratic-spectacular regime' is itself a source of hope because, given that the spectacle has alienated humans by appropriating language, then the realization of 'our vital dwelling' in language, as well as the recuperation of communication will enable reconnecting with others.

One might ask Agamben how the formation of a community that does not operate with the logic of inclusion or exclusion will be brought about. In a sense, ten Bos argues, his account has the hallmarks of a prophetic discourse in that it announces a community that is yet to come. However, he qualifies this claim for the sense of prophecy in Agamben, which is different from traditional prophetic accounts that either await the future arrival of what has been prophesized or consider the present as the fulfilment of the prophecy. On ten Bos's account, it is better to think of Agamben as the prophet who condemns the failings of the present so as to open up or carve out a space and time for the future (2005: 21). In this sense, the 'coming community' is crucially linked to the emphasis, evident throughout Agamben's writings, on the potential and the possible. Unlike those prophets who were certain of what would unfold in the future, for Agamben, it is the present that has within it the potential or the possibility – or not – for the actualization of the 'coming community'.

The communicability of the 'coming community'

In his account of the emergence of the coming community, Agamben discusses the relation between the 'planetary bourgeois' and communication so as to justify the claim that they constitute the basis for a community of singular beings. There are two connected reasons for his claim:

(a) The first claim is that the 'planetary bourgeois' is the dominant and victorious social class since the class struggles of the past are over. Given that they are the only class left, they no longer need markers with which to identify themselves. As any markers of belonging have been superseded, there is, crucially, no identity for them to express or communicate, and this is why the 'difference of language, of dialect, of ways of life, of character, of custom, and even the physical particularities of each person – has lost any meaning for them and any capacity for expression and communication' (1993: 63–64).

(b) the second connects the aforementioned sense of loss: given the bourgeois individuality and the expression of this individuality – self-expression – as a supreme value, Agamben points out that the fact of death disrupts the glorification of the individual by constantly reminding the bourgeois that the individual is nothing. The solution is not to continue to search for a proper identity, but rather 'for the first time enter into a community without presup-

> positions and without subjects, into a communication without the incommunicable' (1993: 65). The incommunicable refers to the bourgeois notion of the individual as a unique and fathomless being, unable to communicate their individuality.

With the demise of this bourgeois notion of communication, a view that Agamben adopts from Benjamin on language as instrumental, the potential for authentic communication grounded in communicability and consequently for a kind of communication without subjects defined according to communal markers of identity, then Agamben is hopeful that something new might be created. Ten Bos extrapolates an interesting observation on the dynamics of global capitalism that is not interested in national, religious or political identities so long as citizens continue to consume. But, the question he raises is whether the bourgeois – as Agamben's hope – can bring about the 'coming community' since 'the bourgeois consumer is so essential to global capitalism' (ten Bos 2005: 22).

On the question of how communication relates to the 'coming community', Agamben distinguishes between the notion of 'pure' language and 'pure' communication to an 'impure' language. While the latter refers to language when it is used to talk about the world or the contents of the mind, a language that communicates what is common, it is the former as the experience of communication itself that is important, as an experience of the thatness of communication:

> [T]he era in which we live is also that in which for the first time it is possible for humans to experience their own linguistic being – not this or that content of language, but language *itself*, not this or that true proposition, but the very fact that one speaks.
> (1993: 83, original emphasis)

There is a further and crucial conceptual link between the concept of communicability and Agamben's account of the concept of potentiality. In his analysis of potentiality, Agamben points to the usually neglected aspect of potentiality, where the potential to do something is not actualized, always remaining in abeyance. While this formulation of potentiality relies upon the classical Aristotelian distinction between the actual and the potential, Agamben is more interested in the analysis of potentiality as both the potential to do as well and the potential not to do something. While it might seem that there is an equivalence between doing and not doing, Agamben points out that the relation between the two is asymmetrical in that while the former finds its fulfilment in its actualization, this movement does not nullify the potential to not do: in its actualization the potential not to do is still there but 'suspended'. The non-actualization of the potential to do something can be seen in the practice of the renowned technical pianist Glenn

Gould, who practised the piano by not playing it but by playing the music in his mind. For Agamben, Gould's 'mastery' was that it 'conserves and exercises in the act not his potential to play [...] but rather his potential to *not* not-play' (1993: 36, original emphasis). Not actualizing one's potential is the default position so that even when Gould was not playing, he remained a musical genius.

Agamben's analysis of potentiality can also be applied to communication, for while all humans have the potential to communicate, it is always possible for humans to not communicate, to not actualize this potential, as when one remains silent. The analysis of potentiality is elaborated upon in detail in *Potentialities,* where Agamben distinguishes between a generic sense of potential and a specific one. When this applies to language, the generic sense of potential is that of acquiring a language, while the specific potential refers to the use or not use of language to communicate. But, '[i]t is perfectly possible to refuse to speak or to use language in a way that doesn't allow it to communicate, that renders it inoperative' (Murray 2010: 47).

But the decision to not communicate has powerful repercussions, as Agamben's analysis of Herman Melville's celebrated short story called 'Bartleby, the Scrivener' demonstrates. Bartleby was a writer or scrivener who was tasked with was that of copying documents in a legal office, but when asked to perform other tasks, such as comparing documents, he solemnly repeated, 'I would prefer not to', a reply that infuriated his employer. With time, he refuses to perform his copying duties and is unable to deal with him; his employer abandons the building forever. The new tenants ask Bartleby to leave the building, to which he once again replies, 'I would prefer not to'. He is eventually arrested as a vagrant and imprisoned where he 'prefers not to eat'. We are subsequently informed of his death by the narrator. The mysteriousness of Bartleby's act of civil disobedience affects a 'dual disobedience' in that he both refuses to write and he also refuses to explain his behaviour. It is a case of resisting not just one feature of the system but the system as a whole. For Agamben, it is the framework of potential and possibility that enables one to understand this literary figure rather than any psychological or biographical explanation. As already discussed, potentiality allows one to do something but also to not do it and Bartleby, in effect, preferred not to activate his potentiality. It is important to realize that Bartleby is not saying No to the requests made of him but is expressing a preference. It was possible for him to comply with what was asked of him, but because his answer cannot be categorized as either a yes or a no, obedience or disobedience to the law/authority, Bartleby's preference, in effect, is a paradigm case of disrupting the structure of the law. Agamben's articulation of potentiality as doing/not doing is part of his strategy for disrupting the forces of authority and control (Murray 2010: 46–49).

The question that remains is that of connecting communicability with that of the 'whatever singular'. By way of illustrating what a 'politics to whatever singularity' might be like, Agamben reminds us of the Tiananmen demonstrations. This politics situates a humanity that is both united by virtue of its communicability and its opposition to the State: '[w]hatever singularity, which wants to appropriate belonging itself, its own being-in-language and thus rejects all identity and every condition of belonging, is the principal enemy of the State' (1993: 87).

Agamben singles out the demonstrators in Tiananmen protests as a concrete example of singularities connecting together against the Chinese authorities. The protests exemplify what Devadas and Mummery suggest is an innovative way of thinking about the community as 'a shift in the way in which we might mobilise the community as a means of rethinking the terms of solidarity' (Devadas and Mummery 2007: 1). Agamben's argument is that the State can accept an opposition that has specific proposals because by identifying and categorizing the issues raised by the opposition, it will be able to domesticate the opposition. On the other hand, the State will resist and resort to various violent strategies when an opposition refuses to be categorized and refuses 'any representable identity'. This refusal of the preconditions for 'playing' the political game is, in effect, a direct threat to the existence of the State itself. For the authorities, this is unacceptable, and it explains why, as Agamben reminds us, 'sooner or later, the tanks will appear' (1993: 87).

If we connect Agamben's account of potentiality with that of communication, it is clear from his account that the coming community is not a final end state, not the actualization sometime in the future of its present potential. The 'coming community' is always already present as a possibility, but only insofar as it can be thought of as a community 'without representation or possible description' (1993: 24–25). Given its lack of representable identity, the realization of the shared fact of its communicability will bring together this community. The value of Agamben's analysis is that while it is critical of community as traditionally formulated, it prepares the way for an alternative account of community as an activity, as a practice that is constantly at work to render the attempts at closing or unifying the community through a common set of markers of identity as unworkable. The emphasis on community as an activity and work shows that Agamben's articulation of community is not something that will happen automatically but rather something that has to be worked at. It constitutes a task of the utmost importance, and if humanity is to be saved for Agamben, the question of the coming community is 'the political task of our generation' (1993: 65).

Conclusion

The originality of Agamben's thinking on community is that of rejecting the 'traditional' view of a community as a shared form of life within which members belong by virtue of fulfilling certain conditions, proposing instead a networked model of singularities that connect with each other on the basis of the inherent human possibility of communication. It is this networked model of singularities that form and de-form themselves according to the exigencies of the situation that constitute a community. It is clear that for Agamben, it is the possibility of communication – what he calls 'communicability' – that opens up the space for the formation of a community that does not cohere around a shared identity.

6

Nancy on Community as 'Exposure'

Introduction

For Nancy, responding to his historical situation, the question of community requires rethinking, and this chapter will focus on perhaps his most celebrated text on the question of community, namely, *The Inoperative Community* (1991). It is not the only text where he examines the question of community and, over the years, has published much and also introduced a number of terminological changes in his discussion on the community such that following *The Inoperative Community,* the term 'community' is replaced in *Being Singular Plural* (2000), with 'being-with' and 'being-together', which he deploys to articulate an ontology of the common. In addition, the debate on community initiated by Nancy was also furthered by Blanchot, whose text, *The Unavowable Community* (1988), is a response to Nancy and one that Nancy, in turn, responds to.

In this chapter, I will introduce the background to Nancy's engagement with the concept of community, which for communitarians is framed as something that has been 'lost' and follow this by examining one of the key influences upon Nancy in this text, namely Bataille, whose role is fundamental in rethinking the relationship between communication and community. The following sections examine Nancy's critique of the question of identity and his positive thesis on community as composed of singularities. The emphasis in this chapter will be on the relationship between communication and the community of singularities.

The 'lost' community

Nancy's re-thinking of community takes as its point of departure the idealized and nostalgic notion of a community that has been lost. This is a frequently repeated 'philosopheme' within the western tradition of philosophy, and while he identifies explicitly Rousseau as one of the first to have expressed this longing for a lost community, a community that is organized around a shared vision of the good life that by definition excludes others who do not share in this vision. The same nostalgia continues to inform some of the debates on community by communitarians such as MacIntyre (2007) and Taylor (1991).

Rousseau's thinking of community is framed as a contrast between a community grounded in face-to-face communication and modern societies where communication is representational in that one communicates on behalf of others. The basis for his valorization of community is that it is the natural way for humans to relate to each other with face-to-face interaction, enabling transparency in their dealings with each other; on this account, the natural state is a pure state. Modern societies, by contrast, replaced the solidarity typical of communal life with a sense of alienation between its members. Given that the feeling for each other was lost with the emergence of modern society, what some considered progress was, in effect, a regression or decline for Rousseau. Iris Marion Young describes this vision of the community as a 'Rousseauist dream' that 'expresses a desire for whom the fusion of subjects with one another which in practice operates to exclude those with whom the group does not identity' (Young 1990: 227). Because of Rousseau's longing and lamenting for the lost community, Nancy considers him a modern. By criticizing modern society and opposing it to an original community, Rousseau is, in effect, acknowledging the emergence of modern society; the debate on the community as he frames it opposes those who lamented its loss to those who celebrated the emergence of modern society.

Although Nancy does not explicitly mention Tönnies, it is clear that the Gemeinschaft-Gesellschaft distinction introduced in the classic text, *Community and Civil Society* (Tönnies 2001) replays the philosopheme that Nancy attributes to Rousseau. His social analysis is grounded in the fundamental opposition between society and community, with several key differences between them serving the methodological purpose of providing a framework for analysing the emergence of industrial societies from rural societies across Europe.

According to Tönnies, members of a community were connected by feelings of intimacy and belonging, typical of families where social interaction was defined by traditional rules and roles provided by religion, family and kinship, which, in turn, generated a sense of cooperation. And just as relations between family members (father–mother, parents–children) constituted the family bond, these relations provided the model for relations outside the family within the community at large (the neighbourhood, the clan, etc.). The unity of the community was maintained through the possession of a shared identity established internally by members of the community.

In modern society, relations between members are externally established through the different needs and interests of the various individuals. These relations were impersonal, and communication was not face-to-face but mediated through multiple media (telegram, the telephone, etc.). The founding principle of modern society was the instrumental use of reason with rational calculation and efficiency guiding interactions between members, and although each member was driven by competitive self-interest, their rationality made it possible for them to create agreements that favoured all and, in so doing, eliminate the social disorder.

For Tönnies, the contrast between community and society was between a rural, traditional society and a modern, industrial one. Typical of the latter was the consolidation of bureaucracies that take over the administration of both government institutions and private enterprises, as well as the differentiation of society in divisions of labour and roles. Based on this entrenched contrast, Nancy frames the debate on community in terms of loss and return.

Bataille and the experience of community

The views on Bataille's analysis of communication are varied: Irwin takes a narrow perspective and argues that communication is the bridge between 'mystical experience and collective religious practice' (1993: 106), while Hegarty's (2000) position is broader in that he argues that communication 'underpins' much of Bataille's thought, and although communication features throughout his texts, the most sustained analysis can be found in *Inner Experience* (1988b) and *Guilty* (1988a). In this section, I will show how Bataille's account of communication links inner experience with the community, providing Nancy, in turn, with the theoretical resources to articulate a different vision of community beyond its customary connotations.

In *Inner Experience*, Bataille theorizes a concept of community that reconfigures the relationship between community and power. While traditional accounts of the community formulate power as a monolithic structure, localized in the hands of one person as the head of that community, his account differs radically in that power is dispersed and spread throughout the community. In the kind of community that Bataille envisions, life unleashes its power through multiple locations: 'The only society full of life and force, the only free society *is the bi-or poly-cephalic* society that gives the fundamental antagonisms of life a constant explosive outlet but one limited to its richest forms' (1985b: 199, original emphasis). As is well known, Bataille, together with others, attempted to create such a community, and they symbolically expressed the idea of community as a site of localized non-power with the figure of a headless man, the figure of Acephale, where the verticality of authority, of power, of hierarchy and the reason is replaced by what Tremblay calls the 'horizontalization of embodied experience' (2016: 47). By removing the head, Bataille wants to make way for the forces of life to be unleashed with community channelling these pre-rational forces towards communion and community rather than allowing for a destructive frenzy. By negating 'authority' as well as 'closure' and 'transcendence', Bataille conceptualizes the community as a negative community (Tremblay 2016).

The title, *Inner Experience,* can be misleading insofar as it might come across as some kind of solitary, mental experience, whereas the opposite is the case, in that inner experience is an opening towards the community, an opening towards the experience of Otherness. The terminology of experience is crucial to Bataille but also requires unpacking: whilst it is usually associated with empiricist philosophy or phenomenology, the term is used to indicate the transformation of experience into categories of knowledge. There is, however, another sense of experience as that which lies beyond knowledge, thought and language and which is not a psychological experience, i.e. something internal to the self. While inner experience might seem like a mystical or religious experience, for Bataille, the main difference between what he is describing and the mystical experience is that the latter is directed at salvation, at some kind of security, whereas inner experience expresses no such hopes; on the contrary, inner experience entails the shaking of one's own existence. Bataille's analysis of the concept of experience brings out two key features: it rejects any goals external to the community itself, such as religious experiences where the self attempts to merge with God; and (ii) it is not a passive experience, not something that happens to the self but rather an experience that de-stabilizes or contests the idea of the self as a substantial entity.

The destabilizing of the self is mirrored in what Bataille calls the contestation of 'the law of language' (1988b: 14). What he means by this is that while language is thought of as having the power to dominate everything or subsume everything within its categories, there is also a beyond to language or, rather, a number of gaps in the power of language. One such gap, for example, is the paradoxical naming of silence: language has a word to describe an experience that lies outside of language, constituting an 'elusive [and] ungraspable part' of language (1988b: 14). Inner experience is the experience of a reality outside the self or of language, and while it can be likened to a force that disrupts both language and the subject, it is not a 'limited existence' (1998: 27) of both. Rather, inner experience is an opening up to an outside of itself towards the community, and what makes the experience of community possible is the experience of communication.

But the experience of communication requires going beyond what is usually entailed by everyday communication. For Bataille, it is mistaken to think of communication as primarily linguistic and then to use language as a model for all communication. Prior to linguistic communication, there is a more general or primary kind of communication that linguistic communication depends upon. This generalized communication can be described as a force or energy that opens and connects things:

> What you are stems from the activity which links the innumerable elements which constitute you to the intense communication of these elements among themselves. These are contagions of energy, of movement, of warmth, or transfers of elements, which constitute inevitably the life of your organised being. Life is never situated at a particular point: it passes rapidly from one point to another (or from multiple points to other points), like a current or like a sort of streaming of electricity.
>
> (1988b: 94)

On this account, generalized communication is a force or expenditure that can account for both linguistic and non-linguistic communication performing, for Noys (1997) the same role as what Derrida would describe as the arche-writing in *Of Grammatology* (1976). There is, therefore, a continuity between generalized communication and more specific forms of communication such that, contrary to the frequent valorization of linguistic communication, there can be no claim that one form of communication is superior to the other: 'It is essential to understand the distinction between two sorts of communication, but this is difficult: they intermingle and the emphasis is not on powerful communication' (Bataille 1985a: 85).

Bataille's account of communication clearly goes against what is generally known as the transmission or linear model of communication; the model is structured along a sender–message–receiver whereby two self-enclosed subjects use, typically, the medium of language to communicate. Nancy highlights the value of Bataille's reformulation of communication as 'the ruin of theories of "communication," of the conventional chatter that attempts to promote reasonable exchange' (1993: 319).

Bataille challenges this model of communication because it presupposes the stability of subjects positioned in a causal relation and prior to language. In a move that anticipates the later structuralist way of thinking about the subject, Bataille displaces the autonomy of the subject by arguing that the subject is constructed by communication: the 'network of communication' pre-exists the subject who is constituted by it: 'Communication is a phenomenon which is in no way added to Dasein, but constitutes it' (1988b: 24). Contrary to commonplace thinking about the subject as the external cause or origin of communication, for Bataille, the subject is an effect of communication: 'I am and you are, in the vast flow of things, only a stopping-point favouring a resurgence' (1988b: 95). This concept of the subject as temporary is directly opposed to the Cartesian view of the subject as foundational. Instead, Bataille thinks of the subject as unstable, as subjected to those forces of communication that undo its ossification into a subject: '[t]hus, there where you would like to grasp your timeless substance, you encounter only a slipping, only the poorly coordinated play of your perishable elements' (1988b: 94).

Communication traverses the subject, linking it to others: inner experience as an expression of communication is one that flows outwards, gushing uncontrollably:

'your life is not limited to that ungraspable inner streaming; it streams to the outside as well and opens itself incessantly to what flows out or surges forth towards it' (1988b: 94). As the forces of generalized communication gush outwards it not only makes language and the subject possible but also makes community possible: 'as subject, it is thrown outside of itself, beyond itself; it ruins itself in an undefined throng of possible existences' (1988b: 61). But as it flows out uncontrollably towards community, it also destabilizes any community that strives to find stability in a fixed identity; if a community defines itself in terms of closure, this would again create another subject out of the community. For this reason, the community itself cannot be defined as a stable or fixed entity but is always opening itself up towards Others.

So too, Bataille's theory of community challenges the Hegelian account of community as the working of the dialectic, as something that is produced by 'Spirit' in what he calls 'the labor of the negative'. Bataille rejects the Hegelian account of the movement of the dialectic as something that works within the community in order to produce it; on this view, the journey of Spirit to Absolute Self-Knowledge necessitates its self-externalization: it can only know itself by way of contrasting itself with something Other. Both of these moments – externalization and recuperation – constitute the process towards the self-knowledge and self-actualization of the Spirit. The motor or power that enables this process to unfold is that of the negative: the Other is the negation of Spirit, and the negation of this negation, in turn, both retains and produces a higher form of Spirit. In terms of community, this sequence can be schematized as follows: the self is opposed or contrasted to the non-self and uplifted into a 'we', and this, in turn, will produce another contrast until all contrasts are reconciled in the Absolute Spirit. During this process, for Bataille, the negative still has a positive role to play, and the question that interests him is: what happens to the negative once Spirit has reached its highest form of consciousness and attained Absolute Knowledge? Is it now redundant, unemployed, or inoperative? This is precisely what he contests: the negative always remains lingering, unable to be re-absorbed by the all-encompassing Hegelian dialectical system. He argues that even if Spirit follows the laws of necessity that culminate in itself, absorbing everything within its system, it is always possible for something to disrupt it. And for Bataille, the singularity and contingency of his own life are enough to ensure that something can escape the Hegelian dialectic: 'my life – or, better yet, its aborting, the open wound that is my life – constitutes all by itself the refutation of Hegel's closed system' (cited in Devisch 2012: 26).

Bataille's theory of community is closely tied to his theory of communication: it is because communication opens up the possibility of Others – of different Others – that this translates into different possible communities. If there is no openness to Others, then how can a community come into being in the first place? This is why, for Bataille, there are no closed, static communities, as these, in effect, prevent different communities from coming into being.

Nancy on community and identity

Nancy finds in Bataille's thought on community an attempt to re-think community as that which both resists the individualism of bourgeois capitalism as expressed in democratic politics and fascist totalitarianism. These opposed and conflicting forces sought control over society in Bataille's times – and perhaps today. But while it might seem that Bataille is a politically motivated thinker, over time, he had given up on political formations as these were only interested in seizing power. For Noys, Bataille argued for a freedom that is 'not affiliated to any politics' (2000: 47), a freedom that would fit into his vision of a community that would bypass these political formations. Noys defends Bataille against allegations by members of the Frankfurt School that he was sympathetic to fascism or that his writings are somehow aligned with fascist thought. Nancy also comments on Bataille's fascination with fascism, but Noys convincingly argues that what attracted Bataille to fascism was the 'intensity' of their ideas of community, but his account of community is precisely the opposite of theirs, given that fascism theorizes communities as closed to Others (2000: 45–47).

Both Bataille and Nancy are engaged in a rethinking of community that challenges the presuppositions that the debate on community has taken for granted, namely the articulation of community around a common identity. For both, the rethinking of community is connected to the notion of communication, with Bataille arguing for communication as a force that opens up to Others, and for Nancy, of communication with Others as always incomplete and transitory.

And yet, despite Bataille's rethinking of community as a communicative opening, Nancy identifies a problem with this account of the relationship between communication and community. When Bataille writes, '[t]o communicate means to try and to establish a unity, to make one of many; this is what the word communion means' (2001: 5), he is, according to Tremblay (2016), situating the concept of communication within the framework of the Christian background of communion. For Bataille, the experience of communication is the experience of bringing together into a community those who share in the experience of going beyond themselves towards others; it is an experience of transcendence but not in the sense of transcending towards another reality. For Bataille, communication produces a 'fusion of the subject and the object' (1998: 9). This is what Nancy objects to: the idea of 'fusion' is a relapse into the nostalgic thinking of communities as 'communion', as bringing together into a shared common-ness. Underlying Bataille's account of communication and community is that of a 'presence-to-self' that produces a community in the presence of subjects. This is the tension inherent to Bataille's thinking of community that Noys specifies: 'Bataille is in danger of taking communication as a moment of fusion where community is produced as present, whereas his own reading of communication is of communication as interruption and the opening of community' (2000: 55). What Nancy wants to think in terms of community is different insofar as the impossibility of thinking of it as closed, and static is the condition of possibility for it to be always open; the relation between communication and community is both disruptive and enabling of community (1991: 27).

But for Nancy, the centrality of Bataille's thinking lies in the way he attempts to come to terms with what Nancy calls the 'exigency' of community: 'No doubt Bataille has gone the furthest into the crucial experience of the modern destiny of community' (1991: 16). Nancy finds in Bataille the resources for an alternative way of thinking about the community that does not succumb to either the Hegelian/Marxist views or conservative ones: a community is not to be thought of as 'a work to be produced, a lost communion' (1991: 19). Both the idea of community as project one works towards, or as a fusion between members will constitute the basis for Nancy's critical analysis of community.

The critical analysis is undertaken in *The Inoperative Community* (1991), a text that remains key in any discussion on community. Within the philosophical tradition, the concept of community has been attributed with connotations of identity, typically formulated in terms of the community as an organic and harmonious unity: 'community is not only the intimate communication between its members but also its organic communion with its own essence' (1991: 9). What the text did was regenerate the debate on community by shifting the terms of the debate away from the question of a shared identity that characterized many previous debates. For communitarians, it is the shared identity that constitutes the social bond. In contrast, for liberals, the social bond is downplayed or ignored to make space for the rights of the individual, typified by modern society. But while for communitarians, a shared identity is a positive feature in that it brings together people with a common purpose by sharing in the good life, for liberals, it is a negative one in that it can be suffocating or repressing to individuals who do not share in this identity.

Nancy's rethinking of community does not involve aligning itself with either the communitarians or the liberals because both presuppose the notion of community as a shared identity, and it is precisely this that he is critical of. The logic operating behind this thinking of community is that of inclusion/exclusion: the purity of a community is framed according to whatever is included within its identity, while the impure is posited as the Other of the community. Because this ideal of community as a shared identity is no longer tenable, Nancy claims that in today's world, we are witnessing 'the dislocation or the conflagration of community' (1991: 1).

Nancy's analysis of community takes as its point of departure the historical context of the 1980s, which saw the collapse of the Soviet Union and the eclipse of Western European communist parties. The demise of communism was marked by the triumphalism of western democracies that vaunted the superiority of the free market political system. However, while thinkers of the left in the continental tradition had done away with certain key Marxist themes – humanism and class struggle, among others – they were reluctant to abandon Marxism wholesale. Given this historical situation, there are two issues that interest Nancy: (a) understanding the failure of the communist ideal as a community grounded in liberation, solidarity, and mutual recognition, an ideal that was replaced by its opposite: individualism and capitalism and (b) understanding what he calls the 'communist exigency', i.e. an originary demand that brings people together into a community. Communism is, at its fundamental level, a way of existing with others, a way of sharing our lives with others. The *Inoperative Community* combines an existential ontology that accounts for the sharing of our finitude with others with a political analysis of the contemporary world liberalism and communism (James 2005: 174).

Given the 'ideal' of communism, the baffling question that needs to be answered is how and why it could go so drastically wrong, culminating in the creation of repressive and totalitarian states. It is this failure that calls for analysis, and Nancy identifies the problem in the way it defines humans as working animals, where the essence or nature of being human was 'defined as producers' (1991: 2). Given the premise that humans are defined as producers, as workers, who create their own community, such a community coheres around its exclusive and shared identity. His criticism of both state socialism and communism is grounded precisely in this notion of production, of community as a 'work' that is produced through the rational work of its members. The word 'inoperative' in the title of the book positions Nancy against this idea of production or work in theorizing the community. But for Nancy,

> community cannot arise from the domain of *work*. One does not produce it, one experiences or one is constituted by it as the experience of finitude. Community understood as a work or through its works would presuppose that the common being, as such, be objectifiable and producible (in sites, persons, buildings, discourses, institutions, symbols: in short, in subjects).
>
> (1991: 31, original emphasis)

The term Nancy introduces to describe a self-enclosed community, a community that is organized around a shared essence, is 'immanence', and he challenges the concept of the 'immanent community' by arguing that it is inherently contradictory. An 'immanent community' is essentialist in that its members belong to a community because they have an identity in common (be it religious, cultural or normative). The logic operating behind immanent thinking is that of us and them, of inclusion and exclusion. Those who share in their identity are included in the community, while those who do not are excluded. It is a community enclosed within itself, a totalizing community that uses sameness (of race or religion, etc.) as the basis for opposing those who are different from it. It is a thinking grounded on the absolute where the absolute is disconnected or in a non-relation with anything else. But, as Nancy points out, there is a problem with the internal logic of immanentism that can be stated as follows: if an immanent or closed community is grounded in an identity of sameness, the establishment of such an identity necessarily requires an opposition, something that it can be contrasted to. The problem with immanentism, as Noys points out, is that its closed, exclusive nature prevents that which makes community possible in the first place (1997: 54). In effect, the shared identity of a community necessarily depends on that which it differs from; paradoxically, its so-called 'purity' needs the 'impurity' of the other. With this logic in operation, purity becomes an impossible goal, a never-ending mission to keep away whatever might contaminate it. This is the logic that he wants to replace in his rethinking of community so that the question of communism is re-framed as a 'community without community [...] that is always *coming* endlessly' (Nancy 1991: 71, original emphasis).

Given this concept of a pure community, it is not hard to imagine the consequences of such a formulation, and repressive regimes have justified acts of terror – Nazi or Stalinist – as part of the process of maintaining the purity of their identity or as a way of achieving their ultimate goals. In addition, while this explains why terror has been used to exterminate those who are impure, there is a further twist to the logic of immanentism. The attempt to safeguard the community by eliminating the Other negatively rebounds on the community insofar as it destroys itself in order to maintain its purity: 'Immanence, communal fusion contains no other logic than that of the suicide of the community that is governed by it'. Members of the community are called to sacrifice themselves for the ideal of their community, with this sacrifice transformed and justified as the higher ideal of a final community that is still to arrive: '[g]enerations of citizens and militants, of workers and servants of the States have imagined their death reabsorbed or sublated in a community yet to come, that would attain immanence' (Nancy 1991: 13).

While immanence is 'the problem of totalitarianism' Nancy does not, by way of reaction, celebrate the liberal-capitalism model of the community as the ideal form of social organization. This is because the social bond underlying liberal-capitalist ideology is merely that of economic exchange with nothing enduring that connects individuals together. The liberal account traces its origins to the Cartesian conscious subject whose existence is detached from others. This is problematic, for by starting from the solitary subject, it becomes impossible to formulate an adequate theory of community. And just as the individual is a self-enclosed being, the same structure is mirrored in the community or the State as a self-enclosed entity:

> An inconsequential atomism, individualism tends to forget that the atom is a world. This is why the question of community is so markedly absent from the metaphysics of the subject, that is to say, from the absolute for-itself – be it in the form of the individual or the total State – which means also the metaphysics of the *absolute* in general, of being as ab-solute, as perfectly detached, distinct, and closed: being without relation.
>
> (1991: 4, original emphasis)

What is interesting for Nancy is that both the liberal-democratic and the socialist-communist models presuppose the same logic of identity, and for this reason, his critique is equally applicable to both totalitarian and liberal political systems:

> Essence is set to work [...] This is what we have called 'totalitarianism,' but it might be better named 'immanentism,' as long as we do not restrict the term to designating certain types of societies or regimes but rather see in it the general horizon of our time, encompassing both democracies and their fragile juridical parapets.
>
> (1991: 3)

The critique of the concept of a community as a shared identity is furthered by Nancy's analysis of the inflection of the concept of community that modernity has framed as a 'lost' community. In this respect, Rousseau is the paradigmatic thinker of the community who valorizes the community as the immediate presence of each member to the Other and of each member as sharing in a common identity, and for whom, crucially, this idealized community is lost with the emergence of society. To challenge the concept of community as a lost one, Nancy starts by inverting the claim that the emergence of modern society took place at the expense of the community. Rather, he argues that the idealized vision of community is actually a retrograde projection: '*Society* was not built on the ruins of a *community* ... community, far from being what society has crushed or lost, is *what happens to* us – question, waiting, event, imperative – *in the wake of* society' (1991: 11, original emphasis). It is only from the position of the modern that the experience of community is formulated as one of the absence or loss of a shared identity. This account is nostalgic in that it looks back to a time when an originary community existed, but that has now been lost. But, as this sense of loss is 'constructed' after the modern, Nancy argues that never actually was such a community and the future for community is one that has no shared identity: 'it is a matter rather of thinking community, that is of thinking its insistence and possibly still *unheard* demand, beyond communitarian models or remodelings' (1991: 22, original emphasis).

The community of singularities

Nancy's account of the community differs in that it takes as its point of departure the idea that existence itself is shared: 'existence is asmuch as it is *in* common' (1991: xxxviii, original emphasis). On his account, just being in the world as existing beings implies being in the world with Others. But he qualifies this claim for it might suggest that being in common necessarily involves having something in common with Others, a shared identity: 'being-in-common is not common being' (1991: 29). Given that there is no common nature that brings together individuals into a community, it might be tempting to think that there is no relationship between self and Others but just a collection of individuals, as perhaps liberals might think. This is, however, not Nancy's position because existence always entails relations between what he calls 'singularities'. The question is: how are these singular relationships established? To answer this question, Nancy turns towards Heidegger's (1962) account of Dasein in *Being and Time* and, in particular, to the phenomenological analysis of Dasein as 'being-with' and as 'being-towards-death'.

Nancy acknowledges the importance of Heidegger's critique of the subject in that it replaces the idea of the subject as foundational, as a kind of substance with an account that positions the subject in relation to other subjects. In reacting to the Cartesian view of the solitary, self-conscious self, Heidegger argued that Dascin was 'thrown' into a world that was itself shared with Others. 'Being-with' enables Nancy to think of community as a community rather than as a group of individual subjects who are brought together by having something in common. In addition, the question of Dasein's death is fundamental to how Nancy articulates the community of singularities. By describing Dasein as a 'being-towards-death' Heidegger highlights the limit of human existence and finitude. The limit that death imposes upon human existence cannot be overcome and is beyond the control or in excess of the subject. And for Nancy, this is the value of Heidegger's analysis: 'All of Heidegger's research into "being-for (or toward-death)" was nothing other than an attempt to state this: *I* is not – *am* not – a subject' (1991: 14, original emphasis). Human existence must be understood in relation to the world and to Others, and for this reason, it is always situated. Nancy adopts Heideggerian resources to develop a non-essentialist social ontology into what he calls 'an originary or ontological "sociality"' (1991: 28).

The problem with Heidegger's account, for Nancy, is that he does not reconcile the notion of death as Dasein's 'ownmost possibility' with Dasein's existence as always already embedded with Others, as a 'being-with-others'. Despite the possibility that someone else might sacrifice their life for someone else, the happening of death is always specifically tied to each Dasein. But by focusing on the death of Dasein as exclusively its own, Heidegger seems to have forgotten the terms of his description where Dasein's existence is always connected with that of Others. Death as both individualizing and totalizing is the limit to the community since it cannot be shared, and the only kind of sharing of death that Heidegger concedes to is tied to the concept of sacrifice. When Dasein gives their own life – for a lover, the state or the people – Heidegger repeats the traditional account of death as a kind of sublimation, as the giving up one's life for something greater. Nancy is critical of Heidegger's account not only because it does not factor in the relation between Dasein and the community but also because when Heidegger discusses this relation, it becomes one of sacrifice.

By framing the community of singularities as one where each is exposed to the death of the Other, Nancy shifts the onus of the question of community towards the singularity of its members. The death of the Other exposes or reveals the Others that constitute the community because the death of Others puts an end to the relation between singularities. When Nancy writes, 'the being of community *is* the exposure of singularities' (1991: 30, original emphasis), he is arguing that what constitutes community is the mutual recognition – the exposure – of singularities to each other, a recognition that is accentuated by the death of the Other.

The singular is opposed to the individual with the individual defined as 'the atom, the indivisible' (1991: 3). Here, the concept of the individual refers to the Cartesian subject as an isolated and self-conscious being. For Nancy, to frame the individual in this way can only come about at the end of a community where the community is prior and self-enclosed such that the individual mirrors the immanence of a self-enclosed community. But because being in the world is not merely a collection of disconnected subjects, Nancy introduces the term clinamen to account for the way singularities are connected as 'an inclination or an inclining for one toward the other' (1991: 3). In addition, the clinamen is also 'ecstatic' in the sense that both reflect the way singularities transcend themselves towards each other. With the concept of ecstasy, Nancy argues against the concept of immanence, whether it takes the form of the self-enclosed subject or the self-enclosed community.

A singular being is defined as '*a* body, *a* face, *a* voice, *a* death, *a* writing' (1991: 6, original emphasis), and while each singular being has its own 'markers', it is the singularity of these 'markers' that differentiates one from the Other and exposes them to each other, and putting them into communication with each other. Singular beings are exposed to each other to such a degree that rather than each having an original identity, there is 'a sharing of another singularity' (1991: 40), which means that singular beings are interconnected. Nancy describes this interweaving between singular beings that occurs when 'I experience the other's alterity, or I experience alterity in the other together with the alteration that "in me" sets my singularity outside me and indefinitely delimits it' (1991: 33–34). It is the recognition of alterity, of difference, that puts into play the communication between singularities, that is, simultaneously, the communication of community.

Clearly, communication between singularities is inherent to Nancy's analysis of community: 'Only in this communication are singular beings given – without a bond *and* without communion, equally distant from any notion of connection or joining from the outside and from any notion of a common and fusional interiority' (1991: 29, original emphasis). Unlike accounts that frame communication as having the goal of bringing together, of fusing singularities into a community, he opposes communion to communication: '[i]n place of such a communion, there is communication' (1991: 28). But for Nancy, given that communication is not a process of bringing together, then neither can it work to bring about an end to community; this enables Nancy to claim that community will always remain incomplete: 'Incompletion is its "principle," taking the term "incompletion" in an active sense, however, as designating not insufficiency or lack, but the activity of sharing, the dynamic, if you will, of an uninterrupted passage through singular ruptures' (1991: 35).

Despite the incompleteness of both community and communication, it is communication that enables singularities to interact, share and mutually expose themselves, an exposure that is 'prior to any address in language (though it gives to this latter its first condition of possibility)' (1991: 29). When Nancy claims that community is impossible (1991: 15), this is understandable, given the popular view of community as constituted by the shared identity of its members who communicate to reproduce this identity. But such a community 'would instantly suppress community, or communication, as such' (1991: 12) precisely because it negates openness towards others. In addition, he adds that while what constitutes a community is not a shared identity but a sharing of singularity, this does not imply that a community of singularities somehow attain a higher form of existence: '[t]here is no communion of singularities in a totality superior to them and immanent to their common being' (1991: 28). Singularities do not, by virtue of being a community, somehow attain a higher status that transcends their singularity into a communion; if this were the case would be merely re-iterating the problem of community at another level.

While Nancy continued to discuss the question of being with Others in several texts, the debate on community seems to have receded into the background. This can be in part because the connotations associated with the community became infused with political positions that were inherently racist or nationalist, precisely the essential communities that Nancy was opposing.

Conclusion

The concept of community in Bataille and Nancy takes on a radical inflection in their proposal of an alternative to the idealized vision of a community that coheres around a common characteristic that closes off this community to differences. This view entails a rejection of the idea of community as a work or product, but while for Bataille, communication is prior to the self and opens up to Others, for Nancy, communication and community entail the sharing of singularities, a sharing that is ontologically primary and which, at an ontological level, always already entails being with Others. And because human social existence is ontologically primary, they also share in communication and community, each open-ended and incomplete. On Nancy's account, the processes of communication and community mirror each other such that there can never be an end to communication or community and are therefore always open to difference.

SECTION C

COMMUNICATION AND THE ETHICS OF DIALOGUE

Within the tradition of western philosophy, dialogue or the spoken has been vaunted as the privileged medium for communication. This privileging follows a recurrent pattern: for Plato, it enables participants to mutually engage in the search for truth; for Saussure, it constitutes the object of study for linguistics; and for Habermas, it explains both social order and social change within society.

This privileging has been challenged on a number of counts. For Derrida, it reflects the logocentric and phonocentric bias of western philosophy. By way of countering this, he introduces the concept of arche-writing to argue that prior to both the spoken and written words is a kind of writing that is more originary than writing, and that is the condition of possibility for having a language in the first place. For John Durham Peters, the problem with dialogue as it has been formulated is that it assumes that dialogue enables a meeting of minds in a kind of spiritual connection between persons.

Despite the challenges to the presuppositions of dialogue, there seems to be a wide consensus on its importance. How the concept is defined remains crucial, and for many, it is defined broadly to include both linguistic and non-linguistic relations to Others. In this sense, it is the relation itself that is dialogical. If dialogue always presupposes a relation to Others, then one is subscribing to the view that there is an ethics involved, and the question becomes: what does an ethics of dialogue look like? In the following section, this question will be examined from the perspectives of Levinas, Bakhtin and Gadamer.

7

Levinas on Dialogue and the Ethics of the Face

Introduction

It would be impossible to discuss questions of the Other or alterity without taking into consideration the philosophy of Levinas. Moreover, it is his philosophy of communication, reconfigured to overcome the inadequacies of current models of communication, that enables him to establish ethics as a relation between self and Others. Levinas takes as his point of departure the view that human existence is always already embedded within a world inhabited by and with Others. At its most fundamental level, human existence is a social existence, and while there can be various kinds of relations with Others, for Levinas, the one that defines our humanity is the ethical one. His account of ethics and the ethical relationship between self and Others is brought into sharper focus because this relation precedes any question of subjectivity. This is obviously contrary to the prevalent liberal view of the subject as an autonomous agent characterized by the freedom of choice in the formation of their own identity. But identity has often been gained at the expense of the Other, and Levinas argues that ethics precedes freedom on the grounds that at its basic existential level, ethics is related to justice.

However, it should be pointed out that Levinas presents a very different account of ethics from that which is customarily formulated in theories of ethics. Given the role of the face-to-face encounter in his account of the relationship between the self and the Other, Levinas's ethics can be better articulated as an account that describes what it is that makes ethics possible in the first place. In this chapter, I will start by introducing Buber's account of the I–Thou relationship insofar as it provides the background to Levinas' (as well as Gadamer's) thinking of the self–Other relationship and follow this with a description of his critique of the traditional models of communication. In the following sections, I will elaborate on his fundamental critique of the ontology of the self and then examine his distinction between the Saying and the Said in the ethical relation between the self and the Other.

Buber on dialogue as I–Thou

Buber can be rightly considered as one of the leading philosophers of dialogue. It is central to his philosophical (and theological) vision, and it is no exaggeration to say that he has influenced the thinking of many philosophers, a number of whom are being discussed in this chapter.

In *I and Thou* (1970), he articulates the distinction fundamental to the dialogical relationship. The I is never found in isolation and is always in one, or the Other set and Buber calls the way one connects with the Thou or the It as 'attitudes'. This needs clarification, for by 'attitudes', one should not be misled into thinking he is offering a psychological explanation of how the self connects to the Other. Rather, and fundamental to his overall goal, by 'attitude', he wants to describe an ontological relation between them that is fundamental to how the self exists in the world. To explain the different attitudes of the way the self can exist in the world, Buber distinguishes between 'relation' and 'experience'. The I–Thou way of existence is that of relating to each other, by which he meant that the self and the Other relate with their whole being, i.e. as complete persons. This is opposed to the I–It way of existing that looks upon the Other as a kind of thing, an object that is experienced or perceived. With the latter, the Other is only partially considered in the sense that the connection is based on a specific feature of the Other; the world of experience is a world that reduces the Other to a kind of object that, at times, needs to be fixed. For Buber, 'those who experience do not participate in the world' (1970: 56).

The innovative feature of Buber's dialogical account of the I–Thou is its emphasis on the space in-between both; it is an ontological space that connects the I with the Thou such that they are mutually entwined. The I–Thou relationship is mutually reciprocal, and to highlight his position, Buber opposes feelings to love: with love, there is a reciprocal relation between the I and the Thou, a relation that does not belong exclusively to one of them, but with feelings, there is no such relation because the feelings are within the individual.

However, Buber identifies two domains that have inbuilt structural limitations to reciprocity, namely, the educational and psychoanalytical situations. In the case of the former, while the educator must listen to the student as a complete and particular person (not 'merely' as an intelligent or athletic student) so as to understand them, this process is not mutual since it is not part of the situation for the student to understand the educator. Likewise, in the psychoanalytic situation between therapist and patient, while the therapist attempts to understand the patient, there can be no reversal of the situation as this would not be conducive to the therapy.

It should be clear that he is not using the concept of dialogue in the customary restricted sense of verbal language but as a way of describing what constitutes genuine human existence. The question that needs to be answered is: in what sense does dialogue as relational contribute to a genuinely human way of existing?

Buber's account of dialogue is broad in that while it is typically associated with verbal communication, he maintains that dialogical relations can also occur in other spheres, such as the relation to the natural world, the spiritual world and the human world. While this seems evident in the case of animals, it is not immediately obvious what the response of trees entails; it is much more apparent that animals respond to the presence of humans. In the case of the spiritual world, when ordinary language is used to talk about God's qualities or properties, God is here being transformed into an It. So, too, while God cannot use human language to communicate with humans, they still feel that God is addressing them, and they communicate with God through prayer by establishing a relationship with Him.

In the case of dialogue between humans, Buber is not interested in the content of the verbal interaction, i.e. in what the speech is about, but in the fact that in speaking, one is reaching out of oneself towards the Other. It is speech as connectivity, as the possibility of connection with Others, that he values because it cuts across the space between the I and the Thou.

> The importance of the spoken word is grounded in the fact that it does not want to remain with the speaker. It reaches out towards a hearer, it lays hold of him, it even makes the hearer into a speaker, it perhaps only a soundless one.
>
> (1965: 112)

This also highlights why Buber considers the dialogical relation of the I–Thou as one of mutual openness: both are ready to listen to the Other who is different. The Other is allowed to exist as Other, as one with different views, with a different way of life whether the I is in agreement with these differences or not: to understand the Other does not necessarily mean that one agrees with the views of the Other. This is why, Buber points out, in a genuine dialogue, there is no intention to persuade the Other to accept the I's point of view.

However, while speech is considered by many to be the dominant form of human communication, Buber's relational account of dialogue also includes non-verbal communication. *In Between Man and Man* (2002), he describes two situations, one where two persons meet in an air raid shelter and another where two persons attend the same concert.

> In the deadly crush of an air raid shelter, the glances of two strangers suddenly meet for a second in astonishing and unrelated mutuality, when the All Clear sounds it is forgotten [...] In the darkened opera-house there can be established between two of the audience, who do not know one another, and who are listening in the same

> purity and with the same intensity to the music of Mozart, a relation which is scarcely perceptible and yet is one of elemental dialogue
>
> (2002: 242)

In both these situations, the connection between the persons is not verbal but sensory: in the first case, the dialogical relation is established visually, while in the second, it is auditory. In these examples, for Buber, the sharing of this experience, although brief, is enough for it to be considered dialogical. This opens up the question of whether dialogue is being defined in too broad a manner, with Mordechai (2011) adding that the key to understanding a dialogical relationship is that both persons acknowledge and respond to each other, a feature that is missing from the example of the opera.

Mordechai's discussion of Buber's philosophy of dialogue brings out two interesting claims: the first is that the I–Thou and the I–It describe a 'conflict between two ethical positions', with the former characterized by 'care and acceptance of difference' and the latter by a 'feeling of superiority and a desire to control the world' (2002: 210). While these descriptions fit well with Buber's thinking and while the I–Thou can legitimately be described as ethical, it seems that including the I–It within the sphere of the ethical is misplaced insofar as treating the Other as an It is precisely to be beyond or outside the ethical. The second is that Buber fails to consider another crucial feature of the dialogical encounter, namely, the role of listening. Buber only infrequently discusses this, but when he does, he argues that the conditions of possibility for genuine listening are that the listener understands that the message is being directly specifically to them and that the listener is engaged actively in listening to the message. Given Buber's lack of detail, Mordechai reconstructs a possible Buberian position with regard to listening that ties in with his account of speaking. This reconstruction shows that there is a mutual dependency between speaker and listener, with the listener depending on the speaker to initiate the dialogue and the speaker depending on the listener to hear what is being said. This is why 'in a verbal dialogue, speaking and listening are mutually dependent in the sense that one cannot have one without the other' (2002: 261). Moreover, he adds, given Buber's claim that dialogical relations can also occur nonverbally, then one must also be able to listen, or perhaps more aptly, 'read' the nonverbal signs and respond accordingly.

Buber's account of dialogue presupposes the ontological space of the 'in-between' as the constitutive basis for the reciprocal relationship between the I–Thou, with possible asymmetrical relations derived from the more fundamentally reciprocal ones. As will be seen, while Levinas acknowledges the centrality of Buber to the philosophy of dialogue, he is also sharply critical of his account.

Levinas' critique of traditional models of communication

There is extensive literature on the differences between Buber and Levinas, and Arnett (2012: 140–55) lists Levinas' difference with Buber as (a) a disagreement on the question of reciprocity, (b) a rejection of the Cartesian dualistic presuppositions implicit in Buber's writings, (c) a challenge to the Buber's I–Thou relationship as too 'private' and (d) a rejection of dialogical interaction as the fusion of both.

For Levinas, dialogue carries a different weight than it does for Buber and in his analysis of dialogical communication, Levinas argues against widely accepted theories of communication. On his account, communication is

> not reducible to the phenomenon of truth and the manifestation of truth conceived as a combination of psychological elements: thought in an ego – will or intention to make this thought pass into another ego – message by a sign designating this thought – perception of the sign by another ego – deciphering of the sign. The elements of this mosaic are already in place in the antecedent exposure of the ego to the other, the non-indifference to another, which is not a simple 'intention to address a message'. (1978: 48)

Communication is fundamental to Levinas's reformulation of the ethical dynamic between the self and the Other, and he focuses on dialogical communication, contrasting his account to other theories such as (a) the linear model of communication whereby a message is encoded by the sender, who transmits this message to the receiver, who in turn decodes it to understand the message; (b) the expressive model of communication, with communication expressing an inner truth in the manner of Kierkegaard or objective truth, as depicted by correspondence theories; (c) the intentional model of communication where the speaker intends a meaning as theorized by Husserlian phenomenology, and (d) the consensual model of communication, where the goal of communication is that of achieving a consensus or agreement between members of a community in their attempt at resolving problems, an account that is dominated by Habermas's theory of communicative action.

The underlying presupposition of these theories of communication is that the goal of communication is that of bringing people together in a unity or fusion of meaning: 'if communication bears the sign of failure or inauthenticity, it is because it is sought as fusion. One sets out from the idea that duality should be transformed into unity – that the social relation should end in communion' (Levinas 1996: 104). The problem with this presupposition, for Levinas, is that 'communion' eradicates differences between self and the Other. However, while he rejects these theories, the concept of communication remains pivotal to his philosophy of Otherness.

Paradoxically, what strikes him as important is not the success of communication in achieving 'communion' but rather its failure. The reason for this is that he associates successful communication with acquiring knowledge of the Other, an instrumental view of communication, which is, for him, an attempt at reducing the Other to the same. This is why he writes that '[t]he failure of communication is the failure of knowledge' (1996: 104). To counter the dominance of knowledge as the goal of communication, and by knowledge certainty is assumed, Levinas introduces the dimension of uncertainty and risk to the communicative exchange. The upshot of his position is that failure is inherent to the communicative event, and what this brings to the fore is that for Levinas, the attempt to connect with the Other occurs at an existential and primary level, as opposed to a cognitive one.

> It is not due to the contents that are inscribed in the said and transmitted to the interpretation and decoding done by the other, it is in the risky uncovering of oneself, in sincerity, the breaking up of inwardness and the abandon of all shelter, exposure to traumas, vulnerability.
>
> (1978: 48)

The ontology of the self

While the extent of the relation between self and the Other has been subjected to much critical analysis in the western tradition of philosophy, for Levinas, this analysis has been misplaced because its point of departure has been grounded in an ontology that frames the self as a 'thing' with a specific essence. It is only after this essence has been defined and therefore constituted as an object of knowledge that the further task of establishing relations – ethical or otherwise – to the Other commences.

The focus on the ontology of the self as a thing or a substance translates into what Levinas calls 'egology', that is, an exclusive focus on the self, a self-centeredness that disclaims any responsibility for others. By way of illustrating his claim, in *Otherwise than Being*, Levinas repeats Cain's question: 'Am I my brother's keeper?' to argue that the question itself makes sense of a self that is 'concerned only with itself' (1978: 117). This utterance presupposes two ontologically distinct beings, with one's self located here and another over there, and what this question reveals is that Cain is only concerned with his own self as a self-contained, autonomous being detached from any experience of the Other. It is, in effect, Cain's way of eschewing any sense of obligation to the Other. To counter this way of thinking, Levinas writes that 'it must be understood that morality comes not as a secondary layer [...] morality has an independent and preliminary range. First philosophy is an ethics' (1985: 77). By prioritizing ethics, Levinas is re-directing philosophy away from questions of identity and the pursuit of theoretical knowledge towards questions of ethics and difference.

The reversal of the primacy and dominance of ontology with that of ethics is the underlying theme throughout Levinas' writings. In 'Is Ontology Fundamental?' (1951), while Levinas' overt target is Heidegger's thinking on the primacy of ontology, his critique is implicitly directed at the western tradition of philosophy in general. This analysis is elaborated upon in *Totality and Infinity*, where the critique of ontology is coupled with what he calls the 'imperialism of the Same' (1969: 39). The title of the text is indicative of what Levinas has in mind: totality refers to the ontology of the Same, while infinity refers to the ethics of the Other. The problem with the Same is that it is a totalizing process where it attempts to understand everything by excluding all that is different: 'The neutralization of the Other who becomes a theme or an object – appearing, that is, taking its place in the light – is precisely this reduction to the Same' (1969: 43). In this respect, the Same has been a tyrannical 'force' that has suffocated the Other from the expression of its differences. The tyranny and dominance of the same is an act of violence where the constitutive differences of the Other have been eliminated through a reductive process: to know the Other is, in effect, to reduce it to a set of familiar categories that fix its identity as this or that. Those who are different are transformed into what can be known, into objects of knowledge: the drive to theoretical knowledge that underlies ontological thinking appropriates the Other by eradicating differences. This is what Levinas is calling into question in the tradition of western philosophy.

On the other hand, the infinite, as the 'exceeding of limits' (Levinas 1969: 26) is beyond the limitations necessarily imposed by the categories of the self; the Other makes the self aware that there is more to it than whatever ideas the self might have of it. The role of communication in opening up to the Other is pivotal: 'To approach the Other in conversation is to welcome his expression, in which at each instant he overflows the idea a thought would carry away from it' (1969: 51). The basis of the relation with the Other is pre-ontological; it is an existential relation grounded in the experience of the Other. At this fundamental level of human existence, there is no attempt at categorizing the world into self and Other; the process of categorization occurs later when one starts to provide explanations that adopt a calculative and instrumental way of thinking about the Other. With this mindset, the pre-ontological experience is gone, and, as Levinas puts it, '[c] onsciousness is always late for the rendezvous with the neighbor' (1987: 119). However, in the original encounter, there is something that 'moves' or, in Levinas' language, something that touches the self at a primordial level, something that challenges the customary mode of being in the world, somehow inserting itself in the self. The experience of the Other intervenes and disrupts the normalcy of the life of the self; it is a transformative experience in which the self opens up to the Other as a vulnerable being (1978: 54).

The opening up of the self to the Other is an ethical concern that Levinas specifies with the concept of responsibility: 'the very node of the subjective is knotted in ethics understood as responsibility' (1985: 95). But some clarification is required for he is not thinking of it as a responsibility that arises from rational principles, legal codes or social norms. These are abstractions from the concrete experience of the Other in the everyday world that fail to do justice to the Otherness or singularity of the Other as the 'stranger, the widow, the orphan' (1969: 77) because the Other as the expression of the infinite cannot be addressed formulaically but experienced existentially. As Levinas conceives it, the concept of responsibility is richer in that it is both a response to the Other as well as a caring for the Other. When the self is addressed or commanded by the face of the Other, it cannot respond responsibly: 'To recognize the Other is to recognize a hunger. To recognize the Other is to give' (1969: 75). Moreover, Levinas argues that the responsibility for the Other is not restricted to the present, to the self's current relation with the Other, because responsibility cuts across time to the extent that the self is also responsible for the past. This radical account is problematic for theorists of ethics who find such a concept of responsibility too watered down (Roffe 2004: 37–45).

Given that Levinas prioritizes the command of the Other, the dynamic between self and other is not one of equivalence or symmetry; it is not framed as a kind of mutual exchange but one where the Other is morally 'higher': 'Goodness consists in taking up a position such that the Other counts more than myself' (1969: 247). One does not help the Other in order to receive something in return, either materially, as though one is owed something in return or symbolically, as a way of gratifying the ego. Contrary to the egological way of thinking, the Other precedes and is more valuable than the self in what Levinas describes as 'the curvature of intersubjective space' (1969: 291). The self–Other relation is asymmetrical insofar as the point of departure is always the antecedent Other who commands the self. Such a relation is not just 'a non-hierarchical community' but a community where the self–Other relation is one of 'radical incommensurability' with the other inserting and disrupting the self-assuredness of the self (Roffe 2004: 40). The asymmetry of the self–Other relation has been challenged by Derrida, who argues that merely reversing the priority of the relation does nothing to dismantle the entire interlocking structure of self and Other. Just as the Other questions the self, in the same way, the Self can become an-Other to the self; there is a mutual interrelationship between them.

In his account of the asymmetry of the Other, Levinas introduces one of his key notions: 'The way in which the other presents itself, exceeding *the idea of the other in me*, we here name face' (1979: 50, original emphasis). The face does not merely refer to the physical aspect of the body of the Other, and neither is it a metaphor. The face of the Other presents the Other without or beyond any form of representation or categorization. The value of the face, for Levinas, is precisely that it constitutes the basis of the self–Other relation as an ethical encounter where the face of the Other is an expression of the Infinite as that which resists categorization. Although the self is a limited, finite being, it finds within itself the thought of the Infinite, and it is the face that provokes this thought because it makes the self realize that there is something more than its own categories. For Levinas, the uniqueness of each face signifies independently of language or culture; it signifies in excess of its being represented or categorized: 'The face resists possession, resists my powers' (1969: 197). The terminology of resistance can be misleading because it suggests a power that resists, a power that can punish or reward the self. But this is not Levinas's position: the face of the Other is a call that is both unsettling and disturbing and which, because of its excessiveness, disrupts any 'normal' self–Other relation. Occurring at the most fundamental level of human existence, for Levinas, this marks the inevitable ethical dimension of self–Other relations. By positing the face of the Other as a 'signification', i.e. as meaningful, he opposes the ethical to the representational, so much so that the communication of a content 'presupposes the originality of the face' (1969: 202). It is the face that says something even without using words; it signifies. As signification, the face is without a context in the sense that it antecedes any contextual categorization (as this or that) as well as any forms of cognition; it is because it is beyond these that the face, for Levinas, is truly metaphysical (1985: 86–87). The encounter with the Other is not knowledge-driven but a moral one that opens up to and welcomes the Other.

In an often-repeated example, Levinas describes the original face-to-face encounter as one where the face of the Other commands the self: 'You shall not commit murder' (1969: 199). It is a non-verbal command that is expressed through 'the depths of his defenseless eyes' (1969: 199) yet, despite the vulnerability of the Other, the face of the Other has enough force to prevent the self from committing murder, even though they could. It is, paradoxically, the vulnerability of the Other that paralyses the self. The origin of language is the verbal response to this non-verbal command; it is the attempt to explain and provide reasons and justifications for one's behaviour.

In addition, however, Levinas also introduces the notion of the Other as 'Third Party'. This is the perspective of the Others who are outside the self–Other relation and who, as external to it, do not see the asymmetry of the self–Other relation. The 'Third Party' represents all those Others who are outside the relationship and who adopt the standpoint of reason. However, from the perspective within the self–Other relations, the 'Third Party' is visible, and this is important for Levinas because it means that ethics is applicable to all humanity:

> Yet this apparently simplicity of the I-Thou relation, in its very asymmetry is again disturbed by the appearance of the third man who places himself beside the other, the Thou. The third is himself a neighbor, a face, an unreachable alterity.
>
> (2001: 214)

There are a number of issues with Levinas' attempt to show how the western discourse of philosophy has prevented the radical Otherness of the Other from being presented. Despite his introduction of a number of figures (the Stranger) and terms (transcendence, infinity and metaphysics) to describe the relation to the Other, Levinas utilizes the very conceptual tools that western philosophy has deployed to legitimized the Same. Does Levinas succeed in 'escaping' the totalizing discourse of western metaphysics? Derrida does not think so, and in his close reading of *Totality and Infinity* in 'Violence and Metaphysics' (1978), he exposes certain assumptions that Levinas falls prey to. It is worth having a brief look at Derrida's engagement with Levinas:

(a) The first is Levinas's relation to the tradition of western philosophy. Derrida argues that Levinas falls prey to the violence of metaphysics that his philosophy of radical Otherness was supposed to resist. The problem for Levinas is that his attempt to re-think the discourse of western philosophy without recourse to its traditional metaphysical oppositions – the 'inside–outside' and the 'interior-exterior' (1978: 110) – undermines his original intention. To engage with the structures of western metaphysics, it will be necessary for him to engage with the Greek origins of that tradition and given that the Greek language and concepts determine the discourse of western philosophy, the only option for Levinas is to use the same language even as he tries to overcome it. Derrida asks, 'will a non-Greek ever succeed in doing what a Greek in this case could not do, except by disguising himself as a Greek by *speaking* Greek' (1978: 89, original emphasis). By so doing, Levinas positions himself within the categories of Greek philosophy, with its totalizing discourse and its 'violent' reduction of difference to sameness, the very discourse that the face is attempting to undermine. In effect, Levinas remains embedded within the tradition that he claims to be resisting or escaping from, and therefore, cannot claim to have established a 'non-violent relationship' to the Other because violence is internal to the discourse of Greek philosophy.

(b) The second is Levinas's reading of Husserl's account of the 'experience of the other', where he concludes that Husserl's phenomenology of the Other

> is, in effect, a reduction of the Other to the self (1978: 153). In other words, the Other is appropriated by the self rather than experienced in its Otherness. Derrida disagrees with Levinas's account, arguing that for Husserl, 'the other as transcendental [...] can never be given to me in an original way and in person but only through appresentation' (1978: 154). Derrida's point is that the Other is not immediately or directly present to the ego but only indirectly, mediated analogically through the body of the Other. The Other is not appropriated, as Levinas thinks, by the ego because, for Husserl, although the ego experiences the Other, the latter still has its own world, a world in which they experience subjectivity. And despite the Other as having its own world, Derrida continues that if Levinas were right about the radical Otherness of the Other, then communication between self and Other would not ever be possible. However, this goes against Levinas's thought because for the Other to speak to me, to understand me, and eventually command me (1978: 167), then there must be, in some sense, a way whereby the Other is the same as the self (1978: 159).

There are other questions raised by Levinas's account of the Same and the Other. Grondin (2012: 243–46) asks why Levinas claims that the attempt to understand the Other is, by definition, a form of totalitarianism. Is not the employment of a political discourse too restrictive since it might be possible to understand the Other as a desire for justice? Why exclude the attempt to understand the Other as other? After all, is not metaphysical thinking supposed to transcend the limitations of political interests? Perhaps, Giordin suggests, the totalitarianism that Levinas is resisting comes from particulars with a face rather than from ontology.

The Said and the Saying

The later *Otherwise than Being: Beyond Essence* can be read as an acknowledgement of Derrida's 'Violence and Metaphysics' (1978) and, in this text, Levinas re-configures his philosophy in the light of Derrida's critical interventions. However, while some terms ('hostage', 'preservation') replace others ('presence', 'interiority/exteriority'), there is a continuity in his thought that is provided by his search for a way to articulate an ethical relation to the Other that does not adopt the categories of western philosophy. This articulation is now framed in the distinction between the Said and the Saying.

The Said is the domain of what counts as knowledge. It is the thematic or conceptual aspect that philosophy and language have privileged; it is the sphere of Sameness and identity. Levinas explains the Said by examining the way the formation of language performs two tasks of 'designation', the first consisting of nouns identifying objects and the second consisting of combining other linguistic items to create a world of things, events and relations.

> Language qua said can then be conceived as a system of nouns identifying entities and then as a system of signs doubling up the beings, designating substances, events and relations by substantive or other parts of speech derived from substantives, designating identities – in sum *designating*.
>
> (1991: 40, original emphasis)

This account of the Said is remarkably similar to that of Nietzsche, who in *On Truth and Lies in a Nonmoral Sense* (1989) argues that the relationship between language and the world is a symbiotic process whereby words name things, are then transformed into concepts that are projected onto this world and that ultimately constitute what counts as knowledge of it. The premise of Nietzsche's argument is similar to that of Levinas, namely, that the formation of language entails a process of falsification, for whereas objects in the world are different from each other, the formation of the concept transforms these differences into identities. Reality is therefore falsified, and it is through this process of falsification that objects in the world are labelled as the same, and a system of categorization is produced. In a similar vein, Levinas writes: 'The word identifies: "this *as* that" states the ideality of the same in the diverse' (1978: 35, original emphasis). The consequence for Levinas is that the formation of language generates what we come to know as the world: '[t]he birthplace of ontology is in the said' (1978: 42). The primary failing of the Said is that it does not describe how language connects to the Other.

The Saying provides a richer account of language and communication because it takes as its point of departure the fact that it establishes a relation to the Other; this relation is pre-linguistic and the precondition of linguistic exchange. By taking the Other into consideration, the Saying describes the ethical response to the Other as one of 'sincerity': '[s]incerity would then be saying without the said, apparently a "saying so as to say nothing," a sign I make to another of this giving of signs, "as simple as 'hello'"' (1978: 143).

In Levinas's account, the relationship between the Said and the Saying is inverted because the Said presupposes the Saying for it to be communicated be communicated. This is why the role of language as the transmission of knowledge is displaced by the role of language in establishing an opening towards the Other:

> The contact in which I approach the neighbor is not a manifestation or a knowledge, but the ethical event of communication which is presupposed by every transmission

> of messages, which establishes the universality in which words and propositions will be stated. This contact transcends the I to the neighbor, and is not its thematization; it is the deliverance of a sign prior to every proposition, to the statement of anything whatever. Language is a battering ram – a sign that says the very fact of saying.
>
> (Levinas 1987: 125)

The possibility of a linguistic response to the face of the Other reveals a distinction between the that-ness and the what-ness of communication. As Levinas has noted, the philosophy of language has neglected to take into consideration that the communicative act entails addressing someone with signs: 'Beyond the thematization of the Said and of the content stated in the proposition [the saying] signifies as a modality of the approach to the other person' (1978: 47). It is the giving of signs in the act of Saying that connects the self with the Other that is at the heart of Levinas's account of the relation between self and other. 'For it is a sign given of this giving of signs, the exposure of oneself to another, in proximity and in sincerity' (1978: 56). The communicative act of Saying opens up the existential dimension of human existence; at its core, the relation between self and Other is ethical. And what Levinas calls ethical language is the use of language to describe the originary self–Other relation. His philosophy of communication forms the basis for a number of contrasts: ethics with ontology, openings with closings, and the saying with the said: 'Language as saying is an ethical openness to the Other; as that which is said – reduced to a fixed identity or synchronized presence – it is an ontological closure to the Other' (1986: 28–29).

The analysis of Saying also allows Levinas to reinforce his argument against the idea of the self or the 'I' as a 'thing'. What the Saying reveals as it communicates is that the 'I' is actually a fiction insofar as it can refer to anyone who uses it. It is a place marker that merely positions the narrator rather than constituting a substantive entity. In *Otherwise than Being*, saying is combined with another one of Levinas's key terms, substitution, described as the 'possibility of every sacrifice for the other' (1978: 115). By describing the self as substitutable, he is resisting the notion of a foundational self that is fixed and fixated by its location in space and time. Instead, the self or the I transcends itself towards the Other; by responding with 'I', Levinas writes that '[t]he word I means *here I am*' (1978: 114, original emphasis) with the sense being that the I is transformed into a 'me', a 'me' that stands accused in the face of the Other. This is the originary situation, prior to questions of free choice and consciousness; it is a situation that Levinas describes with the term 'hostage', a term used to show that the subject has no choice in the question of responsibility (1978: 136). The use of such terminology might seem to refer only to somewhat exceptional situations, to events that are quite out of the ordinary. However, this is not the case: Levinas uses the colloquial expression

'After you' by way of example to highlight the notion that the self is ready to substitute itself for the Other and is ready to give to the Other its own place. By substituting the Other for oneself, the self as an ethical individual comes into being, a self that is responsible, and therefore not indifferent, to the Other.

There is, however, as Hutchens (2004) points out, an inherent tension in Levinas's account of the self as an agent. Does the self come into being as a response to the commands of the Other, or is there a self already constituted that responds to the Other? This tension is further compounded by the distinction between the Saying as the 'that' that initiates the dialogue and the Said as the 'what' or the thematic content of the dialogue. For Levinas, the Saying is an expression that obliges the self to respond, but the self does not know what to respond to or what the command is about. So, the problem with Levinas's account of the self is that if there is no already constituted self, then there is no one who can respond to the command, and if there is an already constituted self, then it does not know what to do, an account of the self that Hutchens describes as either 'impotent or vacuous' (2004: 48). One possible counterargument is to agree that the command comes first thereby alerting the self to its ethical responsibility; this, however, is then supplemented by a content. In this way, the ethical relation is inherent in the face-to-face encounter as the space of justice whereby the self is obliged to respond in the only way possible: personally, by considering what is required of it to fulfil its ethical obligation. This is why Levinas, though distinguishing between the Saying and the Said, also argues that they are interconnected. While the former calls the self, it cannot proceed without bringing with it content as this would be similar to talking without saying anything.

But there is another problematic dimension to the Saying-Said relation: if the communicative act of saying constitutes the opening by way of response to the Other, does it do so by utilizing the linguistic resources of the said? For Llewelyn (2004: 119–37), prior to the Saying-Said opposition is another saying, an originary saying that he calls, reminding us of Derrida, the 'archi-saying': it is the condition of possibility that opens up to the Other, an opening described by Levinas in the following way: 'The first word says the saying itself. It does not yet designate beings, does not fix them and does not mean to identify anything' (1987: 125). Although there is a sense whereby the Saying is tinged or contaminated by the Said, this is an unavoidable paradox: 'The correlation of the saying and the said, that is, the subordination of the saying to the said, to the linguistic system and to ontology, is the price that manifestation demands' (1978: 6). To counter this 'contamination' of the Saying by the Said, Levinas introduces the concept of the trace to argue that the Saying does not end up submerged in the Said. The opening towards the Other in the Saying leaves its mark or cuts through the Said: 'The plot of saying that is absorbed in the said is not exhausted in its manifestation. It imprints a trace on the thematization itself' (1978: 46–47).

Levinas shows how this contamination occurs in the discourses of the state, medicine, and philosophy. What he seems to have in mind is the way these institutions function by utilizing discourse as a deployment of power. Rather than following the dictates of logic, these institutional sites promote the universalizing discourse of the Said while marginalizing or eliminating the singularity of the saying. The marginalization or elimination of the Other is a violent act: if the Other cannot be recuperated within the Said, then the Other is 'threatened with prison or the asylum or undergoes the prestige of the master and the medication of the doctor' (1978: 170). Despite this, the trace remains inhabiting the discourse of the Saying; it is the festering wound that refuses recuperation into the Said.

There are also non-verbal ways of communication that highlight the ethical relation to the Other; Levinas draws upon the sense of touch to argue for a non-verbal immediate experience of the Other as 'the original language, a language without words or propositions, pure communication' (1987: 119). He draws an interesting analogy between the sense of touch and language in terms of their proximity: 'in analyzing contact [touch] outside the "information" it can gather on the surface of beings, in analyzing language independently of the coherence and truth of the information transmitted' (1987: 125). Touch is important to Levinas because, as a sensual experience, it is close to or proximal to the Other, whereas the senses of sight and sound of their nature require distance from the world. Despite this difference, touch, on his account, is the fundamental precondition for all the other senses: '{t}he visible caresses the eye. One sees, and one hears as one touches' (1987: 118). Given this 'transcendental' aspect of touch, it might better be called arche-touch in the same way that the originary saying is an archi-saying. Both establish the primary contact that will subsequently develop into the full-blown sensory experience of the world, as well as the linguistic world of the Said and the Saying.

In addition, Levinas introduces the dimension of proximity to account for the existential relation to the Other. However, this requires unpacking: for a start, he is not restricting the encounter with the Other to a spatially close one, though it might also do so. What the concept of proximity does in Levinas's philosophy of the Other is twofold:

(a) it shows that despite the attempts at classifying the Other that is entailed by the will to knowledge, there is always something that exceeds the classification. If reason classifies so as to create the necessary distance in order to pass an objective judgement, then the proximal brings the Other closer by revealing the singularity of the Other. Levinas writes, '[t]he neighbor excludes himself from the thought that seeks him, and this exclusion has a positive side to it: my exposure to him' (1978: 89);

(b) it highlights the sense of intensity and urgency that the address or call of the Other brings to the self. Its intensity and urgency find its way into the being of the self. Levinas encapsulates the contrast between the Other as a representation and the Other as proximal:

> The relationship of proximity cannot be reduced to any modality of distance or geometrical contiguity, not to the simple 'representation' of a neighbor; it is already an assignation, an extremely urgent assignation – an obligation, anachronously prior to any commitment. This anteriority is 'older' than the a priori.
>
> (1978: 100–01)

Conclusion

The writings of Levinas on dialogue, the Other, and ethics have been largely influential in contributing to a major re-orientation of contemporary philosophy towards the tangible experience of relating ethically to the Other. Despite the shift in orientations from the *Totality and Infinity,* with its emphasis on the critique of the ontology of the same and the ethical relation to the Other, to *Otherwise than Being,* with its focus on a non-philosophical space for elaborating this relation, it is clear that Levinas' ultimate philosophical vision remains that of giving a voice to the Other. Dialogue is central to Levinas's account of justice, for it is only in the face-to-face relation that the monologue of the same, as a closed totalizing discourse, can be transcended. The linguistic response to the Other in the face-to-face encounter shifts the notion of transcendence away from any other-worldly orientation to a thing of this world with justice at the core of human relations. The value of Levinas's philosophy is that it reminds us that we, with our inflated sense of self and expectation, are not the sole existing beings in the world and around whom the world should gravitate. Given that his way of thinking runs counter to the times we live in, Levinas' writing comes across as especially poignant.

8

Bakhtin on the Existential Ethics of Dialogue

Introduction

The terminology of dialogue, also known as dialogism when associated with Bakhtin, constitutes a fundamental and unifying thread throughout his writings. Having said this, there is a distinctly marked difference in the way he deploys the concept of dialogue, for while in some of his writings, it is used in the customary sense of linguistic exchange or interaction, it is also, in other writings used in a more expansive sense, metaphorically to account for existence as a whole. In this latter sense, it is being used as a metaphysical principle that explains the world as a series of relations.

In this chapter, I will position Bakhtin in opposition to the dominant theories of language that he was challenging and follow this with an analysis of his theory of dialogue that, in turn, provides the resources for the analysis of society. In the final section, I will examine his account of the relation between the ethical and the dialogical.

Theories of language

There is considerable debate on how to classify Bakhtin's writings, and frequently, academic texts are labelled into early, middle and late writings, with each label expressing a different phase of the relation between the author and the text: typically, the early represents the fresh but immature ideas, the middle writings the maturation of the early texts, and the late writings constitute a looking back. In the case of Bakhtin, both Holquist (1990) and Baxter (2006) opt for this periodization, but Hirshkop makes a strong case for refusing such a tripartite classification on the grounds that some works that are attributed to the early Bakhtin belong to a later period (2001: 21–43).

The difficulties of classification are further compounded when the authority of a text is questioned: a case in point concerns *Marxism and the Philosophy of*

Language (1986), published under the name of Vološinov but which has also been attributed to Bakhtin. Dentith outlines the issues at stake (1995: 8–10) with this text (as well as others attributed to Medvedev), but while the debates surrounding the question of authorship are interesting, though inconclusive, my position is aligned with that of Dentith who argues that 'the content of the arguments far outweighs the interest of the authorship question' (1995: 10). I will therefore follow the customary practice and attribute the authorship to Vološinov. The targets of this text are the theories of language that he labels as 'abstract objectivism' and 'individualistic subjectivism' with the former considered rationalist in approach and is attributed to Saussure's (then) innovative ideas, and the latter considered romanticist and can be attributed to Humboldt, Croce and Vossler.

The goal of Saussure's linguistic theory was revolutionary insofar as he wanted to transform the study of language from a study that focussed on its historical and evolutionary development to one that would be considered scientific. While previous theories of language were interesting, they failed to explain how language actually worked and, for this reason, could not be considered scientific. The influence of Saussure on Bakhtin should not be underestimated, for while the differences between them are frequently highlighted, Holquist (1990: 43–44) alerts us to some of the similarities that commentators have neglected. These are that (a) both take as their point of departure the perspective of the speaker's relation to language so as to conclude that there is an overlap between the individual and the social. Saussure calls this feature the 'inner duality' of the person, while Bakhtin describes it as 'chronotoped' language; (b) both discount the question of time in the study of language: for Saussure, synchrony – or the present state of language – was the crucial feature for a speaker, while similarly for Bakhtin, 'in cognition the time of the self is always a present state without beginning or end' (1990: 44). Clearly then, for both, the key to the study of language entailed focusing on it as a living entity, as a phenomenon that was used by speakers.

However, in his attempt to create a science of language, Saussure shifted the study of language towards the way it functioned as an abstract system that controlled all its dimensions, from the phonetic to the grammatical to the selection of words used by speakers. This was necessary because the sheer quantity of the variations of tones, dialects and intentions that each individual speaker utilizes makes it impossible to produce a science of language. As a result, with Saussure, the study of language became a study of the abstract formal rules that make dialogue possible.

So too, from the perspective of Saussure's linguistic theory, langue, as the social dimension is privileged over *parole* as the individual dimension of language use, with the latter disappearing from Saussure's linguistics. The price for this is that language is transformed into a closed system that ignores speakers and fails to explain the creativity of language users: 'meaningful language creativity, on the speaker's part, is simply out of the question' (1986: 53). Vološinov calls Saussure's theory 'abstract objectivism' because it dislocates language from its context of everyday use, from its social and historical context to focus instead on the systemic rules that make utterances possible.

Vološinov also rejects the 'individualistic subjectivism' theory of language where '[t]he source of language is the individual psyche' (1986: 48). This theory stresses the idea that there is a generative process that enables the production of meaning, with the meaning of an utterance produced by the solitary intending subject; it is mistaken to focus on the psychology of the individual at the expense of the social because '[t]he structure of the utterance and of the very experience being expressed is a *social structure*' (Vološinov 1986: 93, original emphasis). By highlighting the social structure of the utterance, it becomes possible to analyse utterances that reflect social conflicts expressed by a plurality of discourses, an analysis that Brandist has remarked is strikingly similar to the analysis conducted by Gramsci.

Both theories frame language as a relation between the self and the Other from opposing positions: for 'abstract objectivism' speakers are passive, with the system of language outside and dominating them, while with 'individual subjectivism' speakers are in complete control of the meaning as it is enclosed within their subjectivity.

Despite the rejection of both 'abstract objectivism' and 'individualistic subjectivism', Vološinov attempts to synthesize their positive features. Dentith (1995: 26) shows this synthesis: from Saussure he retains the social dimension of language, and from Humboldt he retains the productivity of language, bringing them together to argue that the productivity of language is manifested in the interaction between participants within a social context.

Bakhtin's theory of dialogue

Anyone acquainted with the western culture of philosophy knows that Plato valorized face-to-face dialogue as the form of language use that enabled the search for truth. Even outside the confines of Platonic philosophy, theorists of communication have also entertained an idealized account of dialogue that, as Peters (2001) argues in *Speaking into the Air*, is framed as the harmonious transmission of a meaning or a mental state from the mind of the speaker to the mind of the listener; on this account, the purpose of dialogue is to enable a meeting of minds, to establish a spiritual connection between self and Other that in an ideal world would not need to utilize the messy everydayness of utterances.

Bakhtin is also dismissive of this idealized account of dialogue. While he valorizes dialogue within his writings as central to human existence, the idealized view fails to take into consideration that

> [t]he word, directed toward its object, enters a dialogically agitated and tension-filled environment of alien words, value judgements and accents, weaves in and out of complex interrelationships, merges with some, recoils from others, intersects with yet a third group: and all this may crucially shape discourse, may leave a trace in all semantic layers, may complicate its expression and influence its entire stylistic profile.
>
> (1981: 276)

Rather than a harmonious transmission of meaning, every utterance belongs to a crisscrossing web of linguistic and non-linguistic elements that intersect and clash with each other. There is a dynamism inherent within the dialogical situation that reaches no final state, that finds no ultimate resolution of meaning. As Baxter (2006) points out, Bakhtin's dialogical position is clearly opposed to the Hegelian articulation of the dialectic, where the conflict of meanings is resolved and finally synthesized into a totalizing unity of meaning.

Whereas accounts of Bakhtin's dialogism typically start with the utterance, I will delay this momentarily so as to highlight the centrality of the context or the unsaid within which utterances circulate. For Bakhtin, the grounding of the utterance within a specific context is something that needs to be subjected to analysis since it is an inherent part of the communicative act:

> When speaking, I always take into account the apperceptive background of the addressee's perception of my speech: the extent to which he is familiar with the situation, whether he has special knowledge of the given cultural area of communication, his views and convictions, he prejudices (from my viewpoint), his sympathies and antipathies – because all this will determine his active response understanding of my utterance.
>
> (1986: 276)

On this account, the meaning of an utterance is intimately and directly connected to the non-articulated knowledge that participants bring with them. This is the nonverbal background of the utterance, and together with the utterance, constitutes a unity that both speaker and listener can understand on account of the shared context to which they both belong.

The basic unit of Bakhtin's theory of dialogue is the utterance. In his account of the utterance, Bakhtin displaces the study of language away from the focus on it as an abstract system (e.g. its study from semantic or syntactical perspectives) towards its use in dialogue. But, an utterance is not just the transmission of information or a message from one to the other, but directed by a speaker toward a listener within a context. Given this displacement, the role of the listener becomes crucial.

> [A]ddressivity, the quality of turning to someone, is a constative feature of the utterance; without it the utterance does not and cannot exist. If an individual word or sentence is directed at someone, addressed to someone, then we have a completed utterance that consists of one word or one sentence, and addressivity is inherent not the unit of language, but in the utterance.
>
> (1986: 99)

However, while the addressee is customarily thought of as one who is present in person, engaging dialogically in face-to-face interaction, Bakhtin adds the idea that it is also possible for the addressee to be implied, to be one 'whose absolutely just responsive understanding is presumed, either in some metaphysical distance or distant historical time (the loophole addressee)' (1986: 126). Because the addressee is not necessarily tied to the present, it is also possible for someone in the future to respond to the utterances of the present. Dialogical communication always implies the Other, whether the Other is present, real or absent.

In addition to the constitutive role of the addressee, the analysis of the utterance also entails taking into consideration that

(a) the speaker anticipates the possible responses of the addressee and this 'exerts an active influence on my utterance (I parry objections that I foresee, I make all kinds of provisos, and so forth)' (1986: 95).
(b) the utterance is embedded within a network of other utterances; it is not uttered in isolation but is a specific response to other preceding utterances

> [T]he utterance occupies a particular *definite* position in a given sphere of communication. It is impossible to determine its position without correlating it with other positions. Therefore, each utterance is filled with various kinds of responsive reactions to other utterances of the given sphere of speech communication.
>
> (1986: 91, original emphasis)

The meaning of an utterance is, therefore, interlinked to a network of utterances that enable speakers to interact with addressees; every utterance has an 'implicit sense' that 'is based on the speaker's understanding of what the listener already knows' (Akhutina 2003: 100).

Bakhtin also includes a further element in his account of the utterance; this is the role that intention or what he calls the 'speech plan' in the dialogue:

> This [speech] plan – the subjective aspect of the utterance – combines in an inseparable unity with the objective referentially semantic aspect, limiting the latter by relating it to a concrete (individual) situation of speech communication with all its individual circumstances, its personal participants, and the statement-utterances that preceded it.
>
> (1986: 77)

However, while every utterance is produced at a specific time and space by a specific speaker, their intentions are expressed in the tone with its unique inflections: intonation 'pumps energy from a life situation into verbal discourse, it endows everything linguistically stable with living historical momentum and uniqueness' (Bakhtin 1995: 10). What intonation adds to the communicative act is the subjective and emotional dimension of the speaker to their utterance, and this explains why there can be no objectivity to dialogical communication. By way of example, Bakhtin reconstructs a situation where both intentions and intonations come into play: 'Two people are sitting in a room. They are both silent. Then one of them says, "Well!" The other does not respond' (1995: 3). To understand the meaning of 'Well!' the intonation of the speaker – as indignant or reproachful – entails that the background to this utterance needs filling in. The context completes the utterance so, for example, after a long and brutally cold winter, the speaker says 'Well!' as a sigh of relief since the season is changing and the weather is warming up. 'Well!' works because it is uttered with a particular intonation within a particular situation.

For Bakhtin, the concept of intentionality plays a double role in the analysis of the way dialogical interaction can be explained: (a) as the expression of the subjective intentions of participants and (b) as a sign of the Other. This is how he formulates the richness of the dialogical encounter:

> Language is not a neutral medium that passes freely and easily into the private property of the speaker's intentions; it is populated – overpopulated – with the intentions of others. Expropriating it, forcing it to submit to one's own intentions and accents, is a difficult and complicated process.
>
> (1981: 294)

There is a further and crucial aspect of intention that Bakhtin wants to highlight. The concept of intentionality explains the creative potential of language as dialogue in opposition to a sedimented language. The point he wants to dispel is that just because speakers share an inherited linguistic system of the 'already spoken', language consists of merely sedimented structures that are repetitive or formulaic with no room for creativity. Bakhtin's theory of dialogue explains the richness and creativity of language by adding the participant's intentions to the dialogical context as they communicate. It is the concept of intentionality that shows how speakers are able to break from the inherited structures of language.

The consequence of including both speakers and addressees as part of the fabric that constitutes the utterance's meaning within a dialogical situation is that the speaker cannot claim authority over its meaning. The utterance is not the product of an isolated consciousness that belongs to an individual but the co-production of self and Others. The intersubjective nature of social existence is already reflected in language: '[a]s word it is *precisely the product of the reciprocal relationship between speaker and listener, addressor and addressee*' (Vološinov 1986: 86, original emphasis).

Dialogue as social analysis

The dialogical model also provides Bakhtin with a criterion with which to conduct an analysis of various discourses. A dialogical discourse is one that encourages the cross-fertilization of meanings or, as he later called them, 'voices' with each voice contributing to the meaning of that dialogue; it is a unity of self with Others, of identities in difference. In contrast, a monological discourse focuses on a single authorial voice; it is the explicit denial of Otherness and a denial of the dynamics of communication and meaning. In this respect, Bakhtin 'was critical of efforts to reduce the unfinalizabe, open, and multivocal process of meaning-making indeterminate, closed, totalizing ways' (Baxter 2006: 102). Monological discourses are, at times, institutional and frequently official ones. They are exemplified in totalitarian systems that attempt to deny the singularity of the individual in favour of the collective; in these systems, only official discourses that are considered representative of the collective are permitted.

In *Problems of Dostoevsky's Poetics* (1984), Bakhtin uses the criterion of dialogue to analyse (a) the novel and (b) the medieval carnival. Unlike the epic and the poem, the novel constitutes the genre that creates the broadest possible number of voices. For Bakhtin, the writings of Dostoevsky are exemplary of this kind of writing, for he allows his voice as an author to be differentiated from the voices of his characters, adding it to the plurality of voices that interact in the text. The text remains a field of dialogical forces with no final resolution of these voices into a singular master voice. So, too, the plurality of voices that are found in Dostoevsky can be contrasted to Tolstoy's nomological view, where all points of view are subsumed to the authorial voice of the narrator. 'The monologue pretends to be the *ultimate word*' (1984: 293, original emphasis). The valorization of the dialogical is not restricted to textual analysis: for Bakhtin,

> [t]he dialogic nature of consciousness, the dialogic nature of human life itself. The single adequate form for *verbally expressing* authentic human life is the *open-ended dialogue*. Life by its very nature is dialogic. To live means to participate in dialogue: to ask questions, to heed, to respond, to agree, and so forth.
>
> (1984: 293, original emphasis)

The medieval carnival constitutes the Other area of study in which dialogue was allowed to proliferate because it provided a space where customary day-to-day rituals and social hierarchies were suspended. The carnivalesque was a complete disruption of singular authority with its (albeit) temporary proliferation of voices: '[a]ll *distance* between people is suspended, and a special carnival category goes into effect: *free and familiar contact among people*' (1984: 123, original emphasis).

A number of questions arise from Bakhtin's social analysis: (a) firstly, if the analysis of monologic discourse is directed at the way power is maintained in institutional and ideological regimes, then it is also possible to analyse the carnivalesque from the perspective of its power dynamics. However, while the carnivalesque might be considered a destabilization of power relations, this analysis is limited insofar as the power relations that structure the community before the carnival return to their original constitution once it is over; (b) secondly, it has been pointed out (Lodge cited in Womack 2011: 52) that if language is entirely dialogue, then how can Bakhtin oppose dialogue to monologue? Dialogue cannot be used to explain all language use on the one hand and, at the same time, be used to exclude or oppose monologue, which is also a type of language use. Womack defends Bakhtin's position, suggesting that while dialogue is indeed the expression of many voices, it is also possible that some voices attempt to stifle others; in other words, monologic discourse is the attempt to prevent dialogic discourse. In addition, Holquist suggests that Bakhtin does not seem to take monologic discourse as something real but rather 'a logical construct necessary to understand the working of dialogue' (1990: 57).

Ethical dialogism

Holquist (1990: 39–64) raises the following question: is dialogue a metaphor that Bakhtin projects from the linguistic to the non-linguistic world? Or is the non-linguistic world dialogical, and this metaphysics is projected onto the world of human linguistic interaction? The difficulty with this occurs when one of the two positions is given primacy, and the point Holquist makes that this is not the way to understand Bakhtin for this kind of thinking operates with a logic of exclusion, whereas Bakhtin's thinking is inclusive, operating with a logic of both/and. This insight is crucial in that it enables Bakhtin to move beyond the customary binary oppositions that characterize much of western philosophical thought.

Bakhtin's dialogism involves both its literal sense as a linguistic phenomenon and its figurative, non-linguistic sense. In its figurative sense, dialogue is deployed as a metaphysical principle of explanation. Holquist writes, '[t]he mutuality of differences makes dialogue Bakhtin's master concept, for it is present in exchanges at all levels – between words in the language, people in society, organisms in ecosystems, and even between processes in the natural world' (1990: 40).

Because dialogism is all-encompassing, it explains why it is deployed as a metaphysical principle: it describes a world of natural stimuli, natural language and social conditions. And one of the ways in which dialogism plays out in the world is through language, 'natural language is only one of several ways that dialogic relations manifest themselves in the larger dialogue that is the event of existence' (Holquist 1990: 40). With human existence the situation of the individual is that of being addressed: they can respond in different ways and in different forms; they can ignore messages or produce a meaningful response that can be an utterance (1990: 46).

Given that the self is born in a world within which there are Others, then self–Other relations take on a fundamentally ethical dimension with the dialogical in its narrower, linguistic sense, as providing an essential link that connects them. In his writings on aesthetics, Bakhtin re-examines the question of the relation between the self and the Other. While taking his cue from Kant's transcendental philosophy or Neo-Kantianism, Bakhtin (and the Bakhtin Circle) does not focus on the typical epistemological questions of transcendental philosophy. Instead, he redirects the focus of Kant's questions (a) by replacing the epistemological question on the conditions of possibility that explains how the self acquires objective knowledge of the world with the dialogical question of how the self establishes relations with Others and (b) by shifting the question of aesthetics as a theoretical activity to a practical one, to an activity that is not detached from everyday life, but an inherent part of it. The clearest expression of the relationship between the self and the Other can be seen in 'Author and Hero in Aesthetic Activity' (1990), where Bakhtin outlines a trajectory whereby from the sense of self as constituted by the Other at a fundamental everyday level, this relationship becomes more complex in the aesthetic act. On this account, the aesthetic is an extrapolation of the relationship that marks everyday human existence.

The emphasis on everyday life, where the relation between the self and the Other is grounded in a concrete situation, raises the question of what kind of relation constitutes the self and the Other. Perhaps the relationship is minimalist, where self and Other exist in a solipsistic world disengaged from each other but occupying the same spatio-temporal location; or, as Bakhtin argues, the relationship between self and Other is mutually formative and transformative to the extent that they are both present within each other. The social and the ethical are, on Bakhtin's dialogical account, inherent to human existence.

An elaboration of the relation between the social and the ethical also requires that the nature of the identity of the self and the Other is established. As a given, Bakhtin argues that in the formation of consciousness, the constitutive role of the Other is indispensable: 'I am conscious of myself and become myself only while revealing myself for another through another, and with the help of another' (1984: 287). What enables the self to acquire consciousness is its spatial location in relation to the Other: as embodied beings, the self's spatial positioning gives it access to features of the Other that are not accessible to them but accessible to the self (and vice-versa).

> I shall always see and know something that he, from his place outside and over against me, cannot see himself: parts of his body that are inaccessible to his own gaze (his head, his face and its expressions), the world behind his back, and a whole series of objects and relations, which in any of our mutual relations are accessible to me but not to him.
>
> (Bakhtin 1990: 23)

The Other brings the self into consciousness by pointing to those features that the self has no access to; the Other sees more that the self does and, by virtue of this process, transforms the self into a conscious self. This process works both ways with self and Other as interlocking states of consciousness. Consciousness is the product of the interaction between the social and the individual. Both filter into each other, with meaning emerging at the intersection between the individual psyche and the social, with the bridge connecting them constituted by the materiality of the sign (1986: 26).

The recognition of the Other as inherently constitutive of the self establishes a specific human relation of mutual concern and responsibility to each other. This ethical relation is the opposite of the dry formalist moralism that valorizes rules above human existence, a morality that is, in a sense monological. For Bakhtin, 'Man-in-general does not exist; *I* exist, and a particular concrete *other* exists – my intimate, my contemporary (social mankind), the past and future of actual human beings (of actual historical mankind)' (1993: 47, original emphasis). It is the fact of our groundedness, of our being in a world populated by others, that explains why we are answerable beings: by answering both to Others and the world, we are transformed into beings who are responsible for themselves; no one else can be responsible for my actions or words. An ethics that is grounded in existential experience cannot rely on abstract ethical principles that are easily used as camouflage or as an escape from one's responsibility:

> A philosophy of life can be only a moral philosophy. Life can be consciously comprehended only as an ongoing event, and not as Being *qua* a given. A life that has fallen away from answerability cannot have a philosophy: it is, in its very principle, fortuitous and incapable of being rooted.
>
> (1993: 56, original emphasis)

The relation between self and the Other constitutes a fundamental backdrop to understanding Bakhtin's writings. It is this relationship of differences that Bakhtin calls the dialogical constituting the space of the in-between. Against this backdrop of differences, I have highlighted the social dimension of human existence that, for Bakhtin, entails an ethical relationship between humans which implies that self and Others are responsible for each other. It is a responsibility grounded in concrete and specific conditions, as opposed to abstract ethical ideals that are dislocated from the context of everyday life and which would be merely a semblance of living ethically.

Conclusion

A central preoccupation underlying Bakhtin's dialogism is the relation between the self and the Other, a relationship that is ethically constituted precisely to overcome differences. What his writings show is that dialogue – both as a metaphysical principle and as a linguistic phenomenon – is a unity of self and Other, of identity and difference. Dialogue as the relationship between self and Other constitutes the basis of his thinking from the emergence of consciousness to the ethical nature of human social existence. This is why the social and the ethical are inextricably entwined: given that existence is always co-existence, the self and the Other are answerable to each other. The self expects an answer from the Other, who in turn is obliged to answer to the self. On this account, there is an ethical dimension in the social and a social dimension in the ethical. Ethical dialogism describes the relationship between the self and the Other.

9

Gadamer on the Ethics of 'Genuine Dialogue'

Introduction

For H. G. Gadamer, the concept of dialogue is central to his philosophical vision. With the publication of *Truth and Method* (2004), his name became synonymous with hermeneutics, but it would be a misleading characterization to think that his philosophy is restricted to textual interpretation. For Gadamer, the concept of dialogue applies both to the interpretation of texts as well as the relation between self and the Other as they are constituted dialogically. In both cases, self and Other are transformed by their dialogical interaction, whether as readers interacting with the text as their Other or as persons in dialogue with each other. This transformation through dialogue is the underlying unifying thread throughout Gadamer's texts. To develop a fuller account of what Gadamer calls a 'genuine' dialogue or conversation, I shall be utilizing the theoretical resources provided in *Truth and Method* as well as 'The Incapacity for Conversation' (1972), published after *Truth and Method* where he tackles the question of whether the increasing role of technology in contemporary life is hampering conversation. As 'dialogue' and 'conversation' are synonymous for Gadamer, I will use each term according to how he uses it in the text under examination.

In this chapter, I will first elaborate on Gadamer's concepts of understanding and prejudice as they are treated in *Truth and Method* and follow this with an account of language as dialogue as well as the relation between self and Others. The final sections will narrow the focus to his account of the 'genuine' conversation as well as the ethical presuppositions for this dialogue to come about.

Understanding

Gadamer's philosophical hermeneutics takes the Heideggerian notions of being-in-the-world and being-with-Others as a point of departure to show that human existence is always already situated and shared with Others. Humans find themselves immersed in everyday life, engaging in a number of practical and social activities, including, perhaps fundamentally, that of communication. Given their embedded situation, humans want to understand Others (the social world), nature (the natural world) and themselves (self-knowledge). The kind of understanding that humans need as they navigate the world is a knowledge of how to interact; it is a practical, applicable kind of know-how that is opposed to a theoretical kind of knowledge, where what is important is using certain methods and following rules of procedure. This is not, Gadamer argues, the kind of understanding that belongs to humans as they go about their everyday lives. His adoption of the Aristotelian concept of phronesis to depict the human practical way of living entails the self-understanding of both itself and the Other, as well as whatever issue or subject matter is of concern to them. What he has in mind is to change the picture of humans as beings to whom understanding is an attribute of human existence to one where it is central to their existence, in effect, defining their mode of being in the world. In other words, understanding is ontological because it is grounded in the existence of humans as they interact in the world. This is opposed to the view that it can be explained as a solitary mental phenomenon, as psychological, in the sense that it can be reduced to an experience that occurs in the speaker's mind. Rather, understanding occurs in the interaction between self and the Other; it is a process that emerges in the space between self and Other, a process that is never final but always open and ongoing. And while understanding is central to human existence, as the self attempts to understand the world and Others, it realizes that there are limits to its understanding. What is revealing about this insight is that this limitation says something to the self so that understanding is also self-understanding (Gadamer 2004: 251).

The concept of understanding requires further analysis, for there are different kinds of understanding. For Gadamer, it becomes, in *Truth and Method*, a question of identifying the specific understanding that belongs to the everyday world of human existence as opposed to the understanding presupposed by the natural sciences. Understanding human existence entails taking into consideration the situatedness of humans as they engage in various practices. On the other hand, the natural sciences attempt to eliminate this situatedness – the context – through the creation of a method that is universal and transcends all contexts. While understanding human existence requires interpretative frameworks, understanding in the natural sciences requires methods for explanation.

The reason why Gadamer elaborates on this distinction is that historically, there has been a tendency to valorize the natural sciences on account of their success in solving problems in the natural world. Its success has been attributed to the following of certain procedures and rules, to the use of technical skills, tools and instruments, and to the acquisition and accumulation of knowledge. Its successful methodology and universal applicability have led to its widespread adoption as the ideal form of knowledge that all understanding should aspire to. By using a method that eliminated any subjective biases, the goal of the understanding became that of achieving timeless truths and objectivity. Interestingly, in the history of western civilization, the rise of scientific methodology has been pitted against history and tradition as sources of knowledge. The irony, for Gadamer, is that that claim to the superiority of the scientific knowledge that is grounded in its own use of a method that is universal and ahistorical fails to notice that the invention of a scientific method is itself historical, a product of western history at a specific time.

The privileging of science is problematic for Gadamer, for it equates understanding and truth exclusively with the natural sciences. It is not a question of denouncing the achievements of science but rather of challenging two commonplace assumptions: the first is that it is only by adopting the methodology of the natural sciences that one can understand human existence, and the second is that only the truths discovered by these methodologies are the acceptable kinds of truth. As a result, Gadamer argues that certain areas of human experience – the arts, the human sciences and language – were excluded from being bearers of truths because they belong to the domain of interpretation and subjectivity. This is why, for example, with post-Kantian philosophy, understanding a work of art became a question of understanding it as the expression of the artist or aesthetic judgments as a matter of personal taste. One of Gadamer's aims is to bring truth back, not only to the arts but to other areas of human experience.

The difference between scientific understanding and hermeneutic understanding can be re-stated in the following way: the former aims for generalization and universal applicability, while the latter aims for the particular, the singular. The understanding that is part and parcel of human everyday existence necessarily involves taking the singularity of the Other into account. Gadamer is inspired by Aristotelian ethics with its emphasis on practical, everyday experiences in which humans learn, from concrete situations, how to live their lives and how to behave in relation to Others. This learning is very different from the learning of rules and proofs that one learns in the sciences. But what the hermeneutic understanding establishes is that given that human existence entails a relation to the Other, then to a certain degree, there is an ethical dimension to human existence.

Prejudice

Given the situatedness of human existence, Gadamer further argues that in the encounter with the Other, participants do not interact as though each comes to the encounter as blank mental slates. Rather, they carry with them what Gadamer calls 'prejudices': by this, he wants to take into consideration the taken-for-granted values and meanings that humans carry with them as they interact in their everyday lives. They are inherited as part of that socialization process that the self undergoes as they learn to live and become members of society. Prejudices operate at times unknowingly behind the back of the person, and this is why a prejudice, for Gadamer, is a 'judgment that is rendered before all the elements that determine a situation have been finally examined' (2004: 273). These prejudices are not a mere inconvenience or incidental to human existence but part and parcel of being human. The sense of prejudice that Gadamer wants to rehabilitate, after the negative connotations it acquired during the Enlightenment, is that of pre-judgements, of the taken-for-granted. While the connotations of prejudice in English are typically negative, Gadamer is not using the term in a judgemental way but making the stronger claim that it is our prejudices that enable us to understand anything at all. We would not be able to understand the world around us or Others if we were not born into a way of life that had already structured the social world into a meaningful space. What this shows is that prejudices are not a limitation to understanding but an enabling condition, a way of opening up to the world and to Others. Prejudices show that when we try to understand something, we presuppose that it is possible to understand it at all. As they interact with each other, participants bring with them their inherited prejudices to their dialogical exchanges. Because participants are born into a context that pre-existed them, they take these prejudices for granted, and while taking anything for granted might not be constructive for dialogue, without these prejudices, no dialogue would be possible at all.

Gadamer also introduces the term horizon to show that each person carries and brings with them a way of looking at the world, a perspective; it is 'the range of vision that includes everything that can be seen from a particular vantage point' (2004: 301). Both self and Other, together with the prejudices that they carry, are situated within a 'horizon' with its specific values and meanings. Given that self and Other, together with their respective horizons, constitute the context of the dialogical exchange, the prejudices of each are brought to light by the Other. And the culmination of the dialogue is the 'fusion of horizons' where the self and the Other understand and agree on the subject matter; it is not the views of one or the Other that dominate but an understanding that is a 'higher universality that overcomes not only our own particularity but also that of the other' (2004: 304).

Given that human understanding is made possible by the horizon of prejudicial understanding and that human existence is always historical, Gadamer further claims that the horizons of understanding are constituted by a tradition. The tradition – which includes the social and cultural background – informs the present horizon of both self and Other. Both are situated within a horizon that is, in turn, influenced by its history and its tradition. Although self and Other are a product of the historical tradition to which they belong, Gadamer adds a crucial feature to his concept of tradition. He introduces the phrase the 'historically effected consciousness' to claim that the role of history and tradition is twofold: (a) first, that both self and Other are a product of their historical traditions; and (b) second, that they are aware or conscious of the effect of history and tradition upon them. This is important as it reveals that humans are capable of reflecting and changing their existence such that the context that humans are situated in is not a rigid boundary, so it is always possible for a horizon to change in the interaction between self and Other.

The human capacity for self-reflection challenges those who maintain a conservative view of tradition. Some, such as Roger Scruton (2017) and Josef Pieper (2010), have argued for tradition as an unchanging body of knowledge and truths, with Scruton justifying the past as more reliable for guidance in the present and Pieper narrowing the concept of tradition to specifically religious traditions. But Gadamer's account of tradition dispels this view: while some might think that participants are passive recipients of their inherited prejudices, in the encounter between self and the Other, both become aware of prejudices, especially their latent ones and can potentially modify or revise them. This, in turn, shows that Gadamer's concept of tradition is not, as conservative traditionalists argue, an unchangeable inheritance from the past but dynamic and open to revision. And contrary to the charge made by Habermas (1995) that Gadamer's philosophical hermeneutics encourages such conservativism because of its valorization of tradition (coupled with a rehabilitation of authority), it should be pointed out that his justification of tradition as the necessary ground for understanding is not an appeal to a blind worshipping of tradition. Hermeneutics itself is capable of critical thinking.

Language as dialogue

Language is fundamental to hermeneutic understanding, for it is the medium that enables understanding to take place. Given that for Gadamer, understanding is linguistically mediated, he then goes on to argue that the nature of language is itself dialogical. As Scherto observes, 'dialogue occurs in language, and that understanding is always mediated by language, which is itself formed in the process of dialogue' (2015: 14).

To understand Gadamer's justification for the dialogical character of language, his account should be contrasted with the various branches of the contemporary philosophy of language, each of which focuses on a specific aspect of language, whether it is semantics, syntax or pragmatics. Language is considered to be representational, with propositions representing facts or states of affairs in the world and with truth established according to whether these propositions correspond to the world or not. Or else language is studied as a tool, as a medium that is instrumental in influencing or manipulating others.

Gadamer's account of language, drawing inspiration from Heidegger, differs from contemporary theories of language – whether philosophical or scientific (as linguistics) – in that while they focus narrowly on specific areas they take language for granted, they ignore the original phenomenon of language, the 'thatness' of language. Its importance is such that it enables the world to 'appear': language discloses the world, and it is by being immersed in language – as fish are immersed in water – that self and the Other can experience their world. The disclosive nature of language is fundamental because human existence is situated in a world that is made meaningful through language, and it is this transformation of the world by language that enables dialogue and understanding to take place. As Gadamer points out, language is true to itself in dialogue: it 'is only fully what it can be when it takes place in dialogue' (1996: 128). The problem with contemporary theories of language is that by focusing on the propositional content of language, they dislocate it from the everyday contexts of interaction. Their account is misplaced because what it takes as prior is an abstraction of language from its more primary dialogical nature. For Gadamer, the prioritization of the proposition is mistaken because: 'Language is most itself not in propositions but in dialogue' (Malpas 2022).

The inspiration of Plato on Gadamer becomes apparent because he conceives of dialogical interaction on a model of question and answer that brings to the fore the notion that language is not an object to be examined but lives the dialogical interaction between self and Other. In *Truth and Method*, the question-and-answer model is used to show the relationship between the self as the interpreter and the text as the Other. But, to emphasize that he is not thinking of dialogue narrowly as a way of literary interpretation, Gadamer argues that this model is itself derived from dialogical exchanges that take place in everyday life: 'for the dialectic of question and answer that we demonstrated makes understanding appear to be a reciprocal relationship of the same kind as conversation' (2004: 370).

Moreover, for Gadamer, what the dialogical exchange of question and answer shows is that every statement is itself an answer, however temporary, to a question. And it is because humans seek to understand the truth of what is said that they continue to ask questions and that the answers they obtain, in turn, generate more questions. A dialogue, in this sense, is infinite: 'there is no such thing as a first word, for every word is itself an answer to a situation, a question of a preceding set of questions; but there is also nothing like a last word either' (Giordin 1999: 228). In *Philosophical Hermeneutics* (2008), Gadamer identifies three crucial features of dialogue: the open-ended nature of the dialogue is repeated, but he adds two other features: (a) its 'forgetfulness' since we do not think about it when we use it; and (b) its conventional nature: language is a social phenomenon – a 'we' – rather than an individual one – an 'I'.

But there is another fundamental feature of dialogue that needs to be mentioned. This is the concept of play: Gadamer's analysis of the experience of playing games as a two-and-fro movement that follows rules, but that is not governed by them; games that are rule-bound but unpredictable since no one knows how the game will end; so, too, Gadamer points out to the experience of playing games where it is not the players who are in control but the game that controls them. In *Truth and Method*, Gadamer applies this concept of play to the aesthetic experience but does not develop the idea of the playfulness of language in the sections following his discussion of the play of art. However, in his later writings, he acknowledges the role of play in dialogue:

> There is the orientation to the game we play with art and on the other the grounding of language in conversation, the game of language [...]. I needed to unite the game of language more closely with the game art plays.
>
> (1997: 41–42)

Gadamer's account of play is intended to counter the idea that the self or the Other is in complete control of their dialogical exchange; what he wants to say is that a dialogue has no pre-determined end because the participants are carried away by it. This is why the play of dialogue is over and above self and Other: 'play is not to be understood as something a person does [...] the actual subject of play is obviously not the subjectivity of an individual [...] *the primacy of play over the consciousness of the player* is fundamentally acknowledged' (2004: 104–05, original emphasis).

Lawn (2001) draws an interesting comparison between Wittgenstein's account of language games and Gadamer's concept of play. He points out that the emphasis of Wittgenstein's account is on adherence to the rules of the language game, neglecting to include that any account of language needs to explain its resourcefulness and its possibility for adaption to new contexts of use. Despite the terminology of 'language game', the later Wittgenstein seems to have forgotten about the playfulness of language games; Lawn writes,

> Focussing the strict rules of the game rather than the capacity of the game, through the two-and-fro-ness of play, to slip from the frivolity to serious and to change unpredictably, fails to make the connection between playfulness and the capacity of language for transformation and self-transformation.
>
> (2001: 123)

What Wittgenstein seems to have neglected, and Gadamer stressed is the fact that dialogue is 'alive' in the sense that it takes place in contexts of interaction between self and the Other; Gadamer's account of the playfulness of dialogue is more preceptive in that it explains the dynamism, unpredictability and creativity of language.

As the self and the Other interact dialogically, they seek to arrive at an understanding about some specific thing: '[u]ndoubtedly the important for *understanding* here is still understanding the subject matter, the substantive insight. It is neither a historical nor a psychological genetic procedure' (Gadamer 2004: 183, original emphasis). This is important because it shifts the focus of the conversation away from the tendency to understand it as the expression of the subjectivity of the speaker, as a mental phenomenon towards its content. Against the subjectivism that might suggest that both self and Other are in complete control of the dialogue, Gadamer argues that there is a limit to how much the self and the Other can 'will' the understanding of the dialogue. There are limits imposed by the subject matter that direct both the self and the Other in the dialogue. By centralizing the subject matter of the conversation, Gadamer provides a pivot that orients the participants in the dialogue, enabling them to discuss and consolidate or revise their views.

In their conversation about the subject matter, Gadamer claims that the participants together reach an understanding that incorporates the views of both. This incorporation takes place through the 'fusion of horizons', and Gadamer claims that '*the fusion of horizons that takes place in understanding is actually the achievement of language*' (2004: 370). This culminates in what he calls a 'higher universality' (2004: 303) that can be achieved and has raised the question of whether what this entails, in effect, is an eradication of differences, where those who are different are silenced or made to agree in the dynamics of power inherent in dialogue. But as Marshall points out, another way of talking about the fusion of horizons that can overcome the asymmetry of power dynamics is that the self and the Other reach an agreement by 'creating' a common language. It is not an understanding of propositions or statements but a sharing of each's respective worlds that culminates in a broadening of their horizons. 'Conversation with another person, whatever the objections or disagreements, whatever the understandings or misunderstandings, means a kind of expansion of our individuality and a probing of the possible commonality we have to which reason encourages us' (Risser 2016: 59).

As they come to a common understanding or common language, the agreement that the self and the Other arrive at is an agreement on the truth of the subject matter. The dialogical encounter between self and the Other discloses a truth that goes beyond and transforms both: '[w]hat emerges in its truth is the logos, which is neither mine nor yours and hence so far transcends the interlocutors' subjective opinions that even person the leading the conversation knows that he does not know' (Gadamer 2004: 368).

Given that dialogical interaction in everyday life occurs between subjects, the question that requires further analysis concerns the way the self and the Other are positioned as two subjects in dialogue. How does one subject break out of their self (as bounded by their ego) to connect with the Other? What is the role of dialogue in establishing the connection between them? For Gadamer, the problem of subjectivity bequeathed to modern philosophy by Cartesian philosophy is that the self is articulated as an autonomous agent dislocated from its context of interaction. The shift towards the autonomous self ushers in a number of consequences: from an epistemological perspective, the subject seeks to acquire knowledge on their own, while from a communicative perspective, the subject seeks to control the dialogue irrespective of the Other, determining its end so as to control it. But as Gadamer's account of the play shows, it is the dialogue that controls the self and the Other with its back-and-forth movements that carry both along toward no pre-determined end.

The self–Other relation

While much of contemporary philosophy has turned away from the Cartesian autonomous subject, the question of elaborating on the self–Other relationship still remains. In 'Hearing the Other: Communication as Shared Life' (2019), Risser provides an excellent analysis of the way Gadamer responds to this question. In his engagement with Löwith and Heidegger, Gadamer concurs with Löwith's analysis of Heidegger's being-with-others as not placing enough emphasis on the 'with' of being-with-others: 'In the communication that communicates something one shares oneself with another at the same time. The authentic meaning of the "with" of sharing is found in the one-another' (cited in Risser 2019: 5). An in-depth analysis of the 'with' is required for Löwith, examining the way it is grounded in social practices, customs, and especially in their communitive interactions.

Despite Gadamer's recognition of Löwith's contribution, he still considered his claims as requiring modification insofar as the way he articulated the I–Thou relations still retained too much of an emphasis on the rationality of each. Because the I and the Thou remain separated and opposed to each other, there is still too much of a gap between them, and this makes intersubjective relations and communications merely a duplication of subjectivity. In other words, the problem with Löwith's account, for Gadamer, is that it does not show any real connection between participants because the conversation between them is framed as two individuated I's trying to reach an agreement from their own ego-perspective rather than as an opportunity for opening up and listening to the Other. For Gadamer, reflection and self-reflection are 'secondary phenomenon, compared to turning directly to some object' (2000: 277–78). As he had argued in *Truth and Method*, the focus of dialogical exchanges should be on the content of the dialogue together with a questioning that is generated by it rather than on the participants.

The dialogical exchange between the I and the Thou is recast in terms of an experience of the interplay between the familiar and the unfamiliar; it is an experience whereby the I encounters something new or different in the Thou. This experience is illuminating, for by exposing the I to the unfamiliar, the I understands its own limitations. The emphasis on experience should be stressed, for the goal of Gadamer's philosophical hermeneutics is to recuperate the sense of experience that had been hijacked by the natural sciences. For the latter, it is the repeated experience of something that enables a law to be established on the basis of the predictability of the experience; in this sense, experience is equated with routine. But the hermeneutic experience is different, for it refers not to something predictable but to something unusual, to the revelation of some new insight. For hermeneutics, the sense of an experience is that of disclosure, where some insight is revealed. For the hermeneutic experience, dialogical interaction is fundamental: 'to the whole of our experience of life and our world, but like no other science – rather like our very experience, articulated in language, of life and the world' (2004: 565). The richness of the I–Thou relations is opposed to the I–It relation that characterizes the world of science and its instrumental relation to the world of objects and nature.

On the 'genuine' conversation

The question of what constitutes a 'genuine conversation' is brought up in 'The Incapacity for Conversation' (1972), where Gadamer discusses the apparent failure to hold 'genuine conversations' in today's world, a failure that might be the result of the ever-increasing reliance on the technologies of communication. By 'genuine conversation', he reminds us of the great masters of conversation, such as Confucius, Buddha, Jesus and Socrates, whose 'charisma is present only in the living spontaneity of question and answer, of speaking and of allowing oneself to be spoken' (1972: 353). For Gadamer, contra Derrida's ongoing critique of the privileging of the spoken word in *Dissemination* (1981), a genuine conversation can only be conducted orally: the spoken word brings with it a non-linguistic context and in the case of the 'masters of conversation' they bring their charismatic personalities to the conversation. To show the importance of the face-to-face as a context, Gadamer contrasts the 'genuine' conversation with the telephone conversation: here, the question-and-answer sequence that is fundamental to the 'genuine' conversation is also present, as well as the two-and-fro movement typical of everyday conversations. But the problem is that the telephone conversation is restricted to hearing the Other, making it impossible to pick up signs that the Other is open to the conversation. The telephone replaces the living face-to-face presence of participants, but it is by sharing each other's presence that 'people foster an intimacy with one another' (1972: 352) that slowly brings them together. During a telephone conversation, the 'sphere of touching, of being attentive' to the Other is key to a genuine conversation; these constitute the non-verbal cues to the conversation that the telephone conversation has eliminated.

In his analysis of what seems like the apparent contemporary incapacity for conversation, Gadamer (1972): examines two scenarios:

(a) letter writing: Gadamer also illustrates the 'diminishing communication' within the contemporary world that has lost the art of letter writing. In the seventeenth and eighteenth centuries, letter writing was an art that required the skill of presentation, empathy or imagination. All these skills have disappeared with the immediacy of transmission and response that modern communication enables, such that letter writing – with the patience that it required – is a thing of the past with the pen being replaced by the typewriter.
(b) the pedagogical conversation: Within educational contexts, there has been much emphasis on promoting discussion between teachers and students, but this has been quite unsuccessful for a number of reasons: (a) the first is on account of the lecturer, who is supposed to encourage dialogue but ends up being the solitary speaker; (b) the second is on account of the students who find it hard to ask questions and challenge the lecturer critically; and (c) the third is with the lecture structure itself insofar as a successful conversation cannot take place with large numbers of students.

There have been attempts to explain the decline in the capability for conversation, and at times, the explanation becomes one of blaming the Other for their lack of conversational competence. Gadamer rejects this, reminding us that blaming the Other is just a way of covering up one's failure to communicate. On the other hand, he does provide explanations for the problem of communication from both subjective and objective angles. With the subjective explanation, a person ignores or mishears the Other by failing to listen to them. With the objective explanation, Gadamer points to the decline of the idea that there can be a common language that unites both the I and the Thou. Here, he is referring to social life in the twentieth century, where the intrusion of information technologies in everyday life seems to segregate people in their own media bubble, such that there are 'objective social conditions that can make us forget how to speak, that is, how to *speak to someone* and *answer someone*: it is this that we call a conversation' (2006: 358, original emphasis). However, Gadamer is not convinced that the capacity for 'genuine' conversation has been lost: he does not subscribe to any technological determinism. In a 'genuine' conversation, there is an understanding between self and the Other that strives for the truth of the subject matter.

Despite this, there are also many conversations that fail to live up to this standard and in 'Human Understanding in dialogue: Gadamer's recovery of the genuine' (2008: 121–30), Binding and Tapp provide a fruitful contrast to what would qualify as 'genuine conversations'. These are (a) an instrumental conversation that considers the Other as a means to an end; the-Thou is treated in the same way as the natural sciences treat objects, i.e. as calculable. In these situations, there is no personal connection between the I and the Thou, but an objective and detached one, with one of the participants dominating the conversation; (b) a 'competitive' conversation: in this case, the Other is a competitor whose sole interest is that of winning the argument, of getting the upper hand in the dialogue. In this situation, the attempt to understand the Thou proceeds from one's point of view. Both of these do not qualify as 'genuine' conversations because participants have no personal connection. On the other hand, a 'genuine' conversation is one where the relationship between self and Other is established in the search for the truth of the subject matter. It should be pointed out that Gadamer, in his later works, adopts the terminology of the 'other' insofar as the Thou had an implicit 'substantialization' associated with it (2000: 282). In the dialogical encounter with the Other, the limits of the world of the self are recognized, and this itself makes it possible to move beyond them. The value of the Other is precisely that it enables the transformation of the self.

An ethics of dialogue

Given the centrality that the role of the Other plays in the dialogical encounter, Gadamer's concept of dialogue ushers in an ethical dimension to the self–Other relationship. As he points out, for any dialogue between self and the Other, trust is a prerequisite: '[s]ocial life depends upon our acceptance of everyday speech as trustworthy. We cannot order a taxi without this trust. Thus, understanding is the average case, not misunderstanding' (1992: 72). What Gadamer is bringing to the fore is the non-verbal ethical assumption that underlies a dialogical exchange; it shows that there is more to a dialogical exchange than following the rules and conventions of language.

An elaboration of the ethics of dialogue that can be derived from Gadamer's account is provided by Scherto. She has identified four areas:

(a) an ethics of openness. The influence of Kantian moral philosophy upon Gadamerian hermeneutics is pronounced in his formulation of the relationship to the Other. This relationship should not be an instrumental one but one where, in Kantian terminology, the Other should be treated as an end in itself rather than a means to an end. The enriching part of the dialogical encounter with the Other is the exchange of differences. The Other brings something new to the conversation, something that one did not know before; otherwise, it would be just repetition, just more of the same. Given that prejudices make understanding possible in the first place, conversation enables self and Others to question or challenge their prejudices. By being open to the Other in the dialogical exchange, the dialogue becomes a shared project, a productive encounter towards which both contribute: 'All that he [Gadamer] asserts is that openness to Otherness calls for one's capacity to attend to and listen to what addresses us in a text or conversation' (Scherto 2015: 15). The implication, for Scherto, is that the self–Other relation entails an element of care since by it is by caring for the Other that the self pays attention to what it has to say. On her account, the ethics of dialogue entails:

(b) an ethics of self-cultivation. Scherto argues that Gadamer's concept of Bildung is central to the dialogical exchange because both self and Other are transformed by it; it has left them with 'something of living value' (Gadamer 2004: 305). The point for Gadamer is that although the self and Others bring their own horizon to the dialogue, and a horizon sets a boundary for each, they are not limited by it. A productive dialogical exchange does not involve a denial of the speaker's views in favour of the views of the Other, and neither does it entail an identification with the Other: it is a two-way interactive process. In the 'fusion of horizons', both learn something new: 'Gadamer does propose a world-oriented ethics of self-cultivation, insofar as *bildung* represents striving for understanding from the perspective of universality through consciousness-elevating dialogue' (Scherto 2015: 19, original emphasis).

(c) an ethics of mutuality. This focuses on the engagement with the subject matter by the self and the Other, who both have a common concern with the questions that the subject matter raises. For Scherto, the ethics of mutuality is specified by what Lingis describes as 'equality and active reciprocity' (1977: xx): 'equality' refers to both participants being interested in the subject matter and 'reciprocity' refers to the mutual questioning by the participants.

(d) an ethics of solidarity. Given the essentiality of dialogical interaction for human existence, the value of the community is prioritized, for it is the context within which humans reach out to help each other. Solidarity is a value that binds members into a community, and Scherto highlights the possibility of solidarity as 'an expression of human bonds developed through a reciprocal engagement with one another in dialogue' (Scherto 2015: 22).

In addition, what I think needs to be emphasized in this account of the ethics of dialogue is Gadamer's claim that listening to the Other is a moral obligation. It has the force of a calling that is imposed on the self: '[i]t is not just that he who hears is also addressed, but also that he who is addressed must hear whether he wants to or not' (2004: 457). There is an ethics of listening at work where the self cannot ignore or dismiss what they are being told because the questions raised are serious ones. Listening to the Other who is different, to the Other who might say things the self does not want to hear, requires that we 'break down resistance in ourselves if we wish to hear the other as other' (2007: 371). And listening to the Other presupposes that one is open to the Other, which also 'involves recognizing that I myself must accept some things that are against me, even though no one else forces me to do so' (2004: 355). In effect, contrary to those who might think of Gadamerian dialogue as promoting a form of domination, it is clear that for Gadamer, there is an ethical relation with the Other, which entails that, at times, the self needs to accept that it is mistaken.

Conclusion

Gadamer's hermeneutics centralizes dialogue as the way language realizes its nature as well as connecting the self with the Other. On his account, the goal of dialogue is that of providing the presuppositions for 'genuine' dialogical interaction. To provide such an account I have taken into consideration a number of fundamental Gadamerian concepts, some of which – understanding, prejudice and dialogue – are derived from his hermeneutic theory. After this, I show how Gadamer applies such concepts to the broader area of human existence, where the relation to the Other, the possibility of a 'genuine' conversation and the ethical presuppositions for such a conversation are examined. What is evident is that if one takes Gadamer's position that dialogue constitutes the means for establishing a relationship with the Other, then how one conducts this dialogue entails an implicit ethics.

Conclusion

The purpose of this text has been to show the extent to which the concept of communication has been deployed to provide answers to a number of philosophical questions. While this has been the explicit focus of some theorists who, coming from an analytic or pragmatic background, have tended to privilege linguistic communication, others have deployed a broader concept of communication in their analyses. Despite their differences, one feature that is common to all is the widespread rejection of the linear or bullet model of communication that had been so dominant in the 1950s.

In the first section, I examined the question of the relationship between communication and intersubjectivity as it is a question that is central to the thinking of Husserl, Merleau-Ponty, Schutz and Habermas. I have shown that for Husserl, the question of the existence of Others becomes increasingly important on account of the isolated nature of the phenomenological subject. While he addresses this question in the *Cartesian Meditations*, he introduces the concept of the lifeworld to account for intersubjective relations. Merleau-Ponty and Schutz are dissatisfied with his formulation and propose accounts that rely more on the lifeworld. This is also the stance taken by Habermas, who rejects the philosophy of subjectivity by centralizing the role of communication in the lifeworld. What this section has shown is that contrary to the thinking that starts with the subject who communicates to establish relations with Others, Others are always already there, so that communication, in effect, presupposes intersubjective relations.

In the second section, I examined the relationship between communication and community, for given the resolution of the question of intersubjectivity, it seemed good to consider the way subjects live together. This, in turn, presupposes the question of how communication contributes to the formation of a communal identity. For Mead and Carey, the identity of the community – with identity defined as sameness – is central to their account. Communication for them, but especially for Carey, does the work of bringing people together to participate in the collective or shared identity of their community. For Nancy and Agamben, the emphasis of their thinking is on differences, so any question of a shared identity is rejected because, by definition, it excludes those who are different. For both, differences need to be considered, and to this end, communication is articulated as 'exposure' by Nancy and 'communicability' by Agamben as a way of thinking of community as a space that opens towards the Other.

Given that the subject lives with Others (Section A) and within a community (Section B), the question of how the self interacts with Others entails an implicit ethical outlook. Dialogical interaction also implies an ethical relation between self and Others. The question that Section C focuses on asks what the ethical presuppositions for engaging in dialogical interaction with the Other are. For Levinas, the return to ethics is the central guiding theme throughout his texts, with the primacy of the self displaced by the Other as the one who addresses or calls the self towards its ethical responsibility. Bakhtin also highlights the question of being addressed by the Other, and in his account of dialogism, he situates the ethics of dialogue within an existential context that focuses on everyday dialogical exchanges rather than abstract ethical rules. With Gadamer, his fundamental concern is to explain the nature of 'genuine' or 'authentic' dialogue, but for this to occur, a number of ethical presuppositions that need to be embraced by the participants need to be in place.

The goal of this text has been to show the way the concept of communication has been deployed in tackling some of the questions that feature within the discourse of philosophy. This contribution has been increasingly recognized within contemporary philosophy, and by using communication as the unifying thread to the elaboration of the questions of intersubjectivity, community and dialogue, this text will hopefully generate further interest in the intersection between them.

References

Agamben, G. (1993), *The Coming Community* (trans. M. Hardt), Minneapolis: University of Minnesota Press.

Akhutina, T. (2003), 'The theory of verbal communication in the works of M.M Bakhtin and L.S Vygostky', *Journal of Russian and East European Psychology*, 41:3–4, pp. 96–114.

Arnett, R. (1986), *Communication and Community: Implications of Martin Buber's Dialogue*, Carbondale: Southern Illinois University Press.

Arnett, R. C. (2012), 'Beyond dialogue: Levinas and otherwise than the I–Thou', *Language and Dialogue*, 2:1, pp. 140–55.

Ayer, A. J. (1953), 'One's knowledge of other minds', *Theoria*, 10:1–2, pp. 1–20.

Bakhtin, M. (1981), *The Dialogic Imagination: Four Essays by M.M. Bakhtin* (trans. C. Emerson and M. Holquist), Austin and London: University of Texas Press.

Bakhtin, M. (1984), *Problems of Dostoevsky's Poetics* (ed. and trans. C. Emerson and M. Holquist), Minneapolis: University of Minnesota Press.

Bakhtin, M. (1986), *Speech Genres and Other Late Essays* (ed. C. Emerson and M. Holquist), Austin: University of Texas Press.

Bakhtin, M. (1990), *Art and Answerability* (ed. V. Liapunov and M. Holquist), Austin: University of Texas Press.

Bakhtin, M. (1993), *Toward a Philosophy of the Act* (ed. V. Liapunov and M. Holquist), Austin: University of Texas Press.

Bakhtin, M. (1995), 'Discourse in art and discourse in life', in *Landmark Essays on Voice and Writing* (ed. P. Elbow), London: Routledge, pp. 3–10.

Bataille, G. (1985a), *Literature and Evil* (trans. B. Boone), London and New York: Marion Boyars.

Bataille, G. (1985b), *Visions of Excess: Selected Writings 1927-1939* (trans. A. Stoekl), Minneapolis: University of Minnesota Press.

Bataille, G. (1988a), *Guilty* (trans. B. Boone), Vencie: The Lapis Press.

Bataille, G. (1988b), *Inner Experience* (trans. L. A. Boldt), Albany: State University of New York Press.

Bataille, G. (2001), 'Socratic college', in *The Unfinished System of NonKnowledge* (trans. M. Kendall and S. Kendall), Minneapolis: University of Minnesota Press, pp. 5–17.

Baxter, L. (2006), 'Communication as dialogue', in *Communication as...: Perspectives on Theory* (eds G. J. Shepherd, J. St. John and T. Striphas), Thousand Oaks: SAGE Publications, Inc., pp. 101–09.

Belman, S. L. (1977), 'John Dewey's concept of communication', *Journal of Communication*, 27:1, pp. 29–37.

Benjamin, W. (2002), *Selected Writings, Volume 1: 1913-1926*, Cambridge, MA: Harvard University Press.

Binding, L. L. and Tapp, M. D. (2008), 'Human understanding in dialogue: Gadamer's recovery of the genuine', *Nursing Philosophy*, 9:2, pp. 121–30.

Blanchot, M. (1988), *The Unavowable Community*, New York: Station Hill Pres.

Brandist, C. (n.d.), *The Bakhtin Circle*, https://iep.utm.edu/bakhtin-circle/. Accessed 20 July 2023.

Buber, M. (1965), *The Knowledge of Man* (trans. M. Friedman), London: George Allen and Unwin.

Buber, M. (1970), *I And Thou* (trans. W. Kaufmann), New York: Charles Scribner's Sons.

Buber, M. (2002), *Between Man and Man* (trans. R. Gregor-Smith), London: Routledge.

Buceniece, E. (2005), 'How can we be together: Intersubjectivity and communication', *Anelecta Husserliana*, LXXXIV, pp. 119–28.

Burleson, B. R. and Kline, S. L. (1979), 'Habermas' theory of communication: A critical explication', *The Quarterly Journal of Speech*, 26:4, pp. 412–28.

Butchart, G. C. (2017), 'Communication and the thesis of intentionality in Husserl, Sartre, and Levinas', *Review of Communication*, 17:1, pp. 56–73.

Butchart, G. C. (2019), *Embodiment, Relation, Community: A Continental Philosophy of Communication*, University Park: Penn State University Press.

Carey, J. (1977), 'Mass communication research and cultural studies: An American view', in J. Curran, M. Gurevich, and J. Woolacott (eds), *Mass Communication and Society*, London: Edward Arnold, pp. 409–25.

Carey, J. (1997), 'Afterword: The culture in question', in E. Stryker and W. A. Catherine (eds), *James Carey: A Critical Reader*, Minneapolis: University of Minnesota Press, pp. 308–39.

Carey, J. (1998), 'Political ritual on television', in T. Curran and T. Liebes (eds), *Media, Ritual and Identity*, London: Routledge, pp. 42–70.

Carey, J. (2008), *Communication as Culture: Essays on Media and Society*, Boston, MA: Unwin and Hyman.

Chang, B. (1996), *Deconstructing Communication*, Minneapolis: University of Minnesota Press.

Cmiel, K. (1992), 'A review of James Carey's "Communication as Culture"', *Theory and Society*, 21:2, pp. 285–90.

Cohen, R. (1986), *Face-to-Face with Levinas*, New York: Suny Press.

Crossley, N. (1996), *Intersubjectivity, the Fabric of Social Becoming*, London: SAGE Publicatons Ltd.

Daley, L. (2007), 'Communication as limit experience', *Contemporary Issues in Education*, 26:2, pp. 75–83.

Debord, G. (1990), *Comments on the Society of the Spectacle* (trans. M. Imrie), London: Verso.

Debord, G. (2002), *The Society of the Spectacle* (trans. K. Knabb), London: Rebel Press.

De Ia Durantaye, L. (2009), *Giorgio Agamben: A Critical Introduction*, Stanford: Stanford University Press.

Dentith, S. (1995), *Bakhtinian Thought: An Introductory Reader*, London: Routledge.

De Oliviera, P. P. (2017), 'From Schutz to Dewey: Communication and everday life', *Estudos em Comunicação*, 1:25, pp. 163–75.

Derrida, J. (1976), *Of Grammatology* (trans. G. C. Spivak), Baltimore: Johns Hopkins University Press.

Derrida, J. (1978), 'Violence and metaphysics', in *Writing and Difference* (trans. A. Bass), Chicago: The University of Chicago Press, pp. 79–153.

Derrida, J. (1981), *Dissemination* (trans. B. Johnson), Chicago: The University of Chicago Press.

Derrida, J. (1994), *Spectres of Marx* (trans. P. Kamuf), Oxfordshire: Routledge.

De Saussure, F. (1983), *Course in General Linguistics* (trans. R. Harris), London: Duckworth.

Devadas, V. and Mummery, J. (2007), 'Community without community', *Borderlands*, 6:1, https://www.thefreelibrary.com/Community without community.-a0169458010. Accessed 12 July 2023.

Devisch, I. (2012), *Jean-Luc Nancy and the Queston of Community*, London: Bloomsbury Press.

Dewey, J. (1929), *Experience and Nature*, London: George Allen and Unwin, Ltd.

Dewey, J. (1938), *Logic: Theory of Inquiry*, New York: Hold, Rinehart and Winston.

Dewey, J. (1957), *Reconstruction in Philosophy*, Boston, MA: Beacon Press.

Dewey, J. (2004), *Democracy and Education: An Introduction to the Philosophy of Education*, Delhi: Aakar Books.

Dreher, J. (2003), 'The symbol and the theory of the life-world: "The transcendences of the life-world and their overcoming by signs and symbols"', *Human Studies*, 26, pp.141–163, https://doi.org/10.1023/a:1024014620368.

Edgar, A. (2005), *The Philosophy of Habermas*, Oxfordshire: Routledge.

Elliott, B. (2009), 'Theories of community in Habermas, Nancy and Agamben: A critical introduction', *Philosophy Compass*, 4:6, p. 8930903.

Frechette, G. (2016), 'Two phenomenological accounts of intuition', in D. Fisette and G. Frechette (eds), *Analytic and Continental Philosophy. Proceedings of the 37th International Wittgentsein Sumposium*, Berlin: de Gruyter, pp. 129–42.

Gadamer, H.-G. (1992), 'Interview: Writing and the living voice', in D. Misgeld and G. Nicholson (eds), in *Hans-Georg Gadamer on Education, Poetry, and History: Applied* (trans. L. Schmidt and M. Reuss), New York: State University of New York Press, pp. 63–72.

Gadamer, H.-G. (1996), *The Enigma of Health: The Art of Healing in a Scientiifc Age* (trans. J. Gaiger and N. Walker), Stanford: Stanford University Press.

Gadamer, H.-G. (1997), 'Reflections on my philosophical journey', in L. E. Hahn (ed.), *The Philosophy of Hans-Georg Gadamer, Library of Living Philosophers, v. 24* (trans. R. Palmer), Chicago: Open Court Publishing Company, pp. 3–63.

Gadamer, H.-G. (1998), 'Culture and word', in *Praise of Theory: Speech and Essays* (trans. C. Dawson), New Haven: Yale University Press, pp. 1–16.

Gadamer, H.-G. (2000), 'Subjectivity and intersubjectivity, subject and person', *Continental Philosophy Review*, 33, pp. 275–87.

Gadamer, H.-G. (2004), *Truth and Method* (trans. J. Weinsheimer and D. G. Marshall), New York: The Continuum Publishing House.

Gadamer, H.-G. (2006), 'The Incapacity for Conversation', *Continental Philosophy Review*, 39, pp. 351–59.

Gadamer, H.-G. (2007), 'Hermeneutics and the ontologcial difference', in *The Gadamer Reader: A Bouquet of the Later Writings* (translated and edited R. Palmer), Evanston: Northwestern University Press, pp. 356–71.

Gadamer, H.-G. (2008), *Philosophical Hermeneutics* (trans. D. E. Linge), Berkeley: University of California Press.

Gilicka, M. (2017), 'Husserl's phenomenological-communicative project', *Lingua Posnaniensis*, LIX:1, pp. 53–63.

Giordin, J. (1999), 'Understanding as dialogue: Gadamer', in S. Glendenning (ed.), *The Edinburgh Encyclopedia of Continental Philosophy*, Edinburgh: Edinburgh University Press, pp. 222–30.

Grinnell, F. (1983), 'The problem of intersubjectivity: A comparison of Martin Buber and Alfred Schutz', *Human Studies*, 6:1, pp. 185–95.

Grondin, J. (2012), *Introduction to Metaphysics: From Parmenides to Levinas*, New York: Columbia University Press.

Habermas, J. (1972), *Knowledge and Human Interests* (trans. J. J. Shapiro), Boston, MA: Beacon Press.

Habermas, J. (1979), *Communication and the Evolution of Society* (trans. T. MacCarthy), Boston, MA: Beacon press.

Habermas, J. (1982), 'A reply to my critics', in *Habermas Critical Debates* (eds J. B. Thompson and D. Held), London: The Macmillan Press Limited, pp. 219–83.

Habermas, J. (1984), *The Theory of Communicative Action, Vol. 1* (trans. T. McCarthy), Boston, MA: Beacon Press.

Habermas, J. (1987), *The Theory of Communicative Action, Vol. 2* (trans. T. McCarthy), Cambridge: Polity Press.

Habermas, J. (1990a), *The Philosophical Discourse of Modernity* (trans. F. G. Lawrence), Amherst: Massachusetts University Press.

Habermas, J. (1990b), *Moral Consciousness and Communicative Action* (trans. C. Lenhardt and S.W. Nicholson), Cambridge: Polity Press.

Habermas, J. (2001), *On the Pragmatics of Social Interaction* (trans. B. Fultner), Cambridge: Polity Press.

Habermas, J. (2008), 'Towards a theory of communicative competence', *Inquiry*, 13:1–4, pp. 360–75.

Hammond, Mark (1991), *Understanding Phenomenology*, Oxford: Blackwell Publishers.

Haney, M. K. (1988), 'The necessity of intersubjectivity', in H. Silverman (ed.), *The Horizons of Continental Philosophy*, Dordrecht: Springer Science+Business Media, pp. 32–59.

Haney, M. K. (2002), 'The role of intersubjectivity and empathy in Husserl's Foundational Project', in A. T. Tymieniecka (ed.), *Phenomenology World-Wide*, Dordrecht: Klewer Academic Publishers, pp. 146–58.

Hegarty, P. (2000), *Georges Bataille*, London: SAGE Publications.

Heidegger, M. (1962), *Being and Time* (trans. J. Macquarrie and E. Robinson), New York: Harper and Row Publishers.

Hirshkop, K. (2001), 'Bakhtin's linguistic turn', *Dialogism: An International Journal of Bakhtin Studies*, 5–6, pp. 21–35.

Holquist, M. (1990), *Dialogism*, London: Routledge.

Husserl, E. (1970a), *Logical Investigations, Volume 1* (trans. J. N. Findlay), London: Routledge and Kegan Paul.

Husserl, E. (1970b), *Logical Investigations Volume 2* (trans. J. N. Findlay), London: Routledge.

Husserl, E. (1973a), *Zur Phanomenologie der Intersubjektivitat. Texte aus dem Bachless. Zweiter Teil: 1921-1928*, Den Haag: Martinus Nijhoff.

Husserl, E. (1973b), *Zur Phanomenologie der Intersubjektivitat. Texte aus dem Nachless, Dritter Teil: 1929-1935*, Den Haag: Martinus Nijhoff.

Husserl, E. (1990), *Ideas Pertaining to a Pure Phenomenology and to a Phenomenological Philosophy* (trans. F. Kersten), Berlin: Springer.

Husserl, E. (1999), *Cartesian Meditations* (trans. D. Clairns), Dordrecht: Klewer Academic Publications.

Husserl, E. (2008), *Die Lebenswelt: Auslegungen der vorgegebenen Welt und Ihrer Konstituin*, Dordecht: Springer.

Hutchens, B. (2004), *Levinas: A Guide for the Perplexed*, London: Bloomsbury Academic Continuum International Pub. Group.

Irwin, C. A. (1993), 'Ecstasy, sacrifice, communication: Bataille on religion and inner experience', *Soundings: An Interdisciplinary Journal*, 76:1, pp. 105–28.

Jakobson, R. (1971), 'The dominant', in L. Matejka and K. L. Comp (eds), *Readings in Russian Poetics: Formalist and Structuralist Views*, Cambridge, MA and London: MIT Press, pp. 105–10.

James, I. (2005), *The Fragmentary Demand: An Introdcution to J.L.Nancy*, Stanford: Stanford University Press.

Johnson, M. (2006), 'Merleau-Ponty's embodied semantics: From immanent meaning, to gesture, to language', *EurAmerica*, 36:1, pp. 1–27.

Keiichi, N. (1992), '"The hermeneutic turn" in Husserl's phenomenology of language', *Human Studies*, 15:1, pp. 117–28.

Keller, P. (1999), *Husserl and Heidegger on Human Experience*, Cambridge: Cambridge University Press.

Lachowska, D. (1980), 'Alfred Schutz's theory of intersubjectivity', *The Polish Sociological Bulletin*, 3:51, pp. 41–50.

Lanigan, R. L. (1988), *Phenomenology of Communication*, Pittsburg: Duquesne University Press.

Lawn, C. (2019), 'Gadamer on poetic and everyday language', *Philosophy and Literature*, 25, pp. 113–16.

Levinas, E. (1969), *Ethics and Infinity* (trans. A. Lingis), Pittsburgh: Duquesne University Press.

Levinas, E. (1978), *Otherwise than Being or Beyond Essence* (trans. A. Lingis), Dordrecth: Martinus Nijhoff Press Philosophy Texts.

Levinas, E. (1979), *Totality and Infinity: An Essay on Exteriority* (trans. A. Lingis), Pittsburgh: Duquesne University Press.

Levinas, E. (1987), *Collected Philosophical Papers* (trans. A. Lingis), Dordrecht: Martinus Nijhoff.

Levinas, E. (1996), *Proper Names* (trans. M. B. Smith), Redwood City: Stanford University Press.

Levinas, E. (2001), *Is it Righteous to Be? Interviews with Emmanuel Levinas* (ed. J. Robbins), Stanford: Stanford University Press.

Levinas, I. (2001), *Is it Righteous to Be? Interviews with Emmanuel Levinas* (ed. J. Robbins), Stanford: Stanford University Press.

Llewelyn, J. (2004), 'Levinas and language', in S. Critchley and R. Bernasconi (eds), *The Cambridge Companion to Levinas*, Cambridge: Cambridge University Press, pp. 119–39.

Low, D. (1992), 'Merleau-Ponty's intertwined notions of subjectivity and intersubjectivity', *International Studies in Philosophy*, 24:3, pp. 45–64.

MacIntyre, A. (2007), *After Virtue*, Notre Dame: Notre Dame Press.

Malpas, J. (2022), *Hans-Georg Gadamer*, https://plato.stanford.edu/entries/gadamer/. Accessed 29 July 2023.

Mead, G. H. (1922), 'A behavioristic account of the significant symbol', *The Journal of Philosophy*, 19:6, pp. 157–63.

Mead, H. G. (1934), *Mind, Self and Society*, Chicago: Chicago University Press.

Mead, H. G. (1936), *Movement of Thought in the Nineteenth Century*, Chicago: Chicago University Press.

Meindl, P. and Zahavi, D. a. Z. D. (2023), 'From communication to communalisation: A Husserlian account', *Continental Philosophy Review*, pp. 361–77, https://doi.org/10.1007/s11007-023-09601-7.

Merleau-Ponty, M. (1964a), *Signs* (trans. R. C. McCleary), Evanston: Northwestern University Press.

Merleau-Ponty, M. (1964b). *The Primacy of Perception* (trans. J. M. Edie), Evanston: Northwestern University Press.

Merleau-Ponty, M. (1968), *The Visible and the Invisible* (trans. A. Lingis), Evanston: Northwestern University Press.

Merleau-Ponty, M. (1970), *In Praise of Philosophy and Other Essays* (trans. W. Johyn and E. J. James), Evanston: Northwestern University Press.

Merleau-Ponty, M. (1973), *The Prose of the World* (trans. J. O'Neil), Evanston: Northwestern University Press.

Merleau-Ponty, M. (2002), *The Phenomenology of Perception* (trans. C. Smith), London: Routledge.

Moran, D. (2013), '"There is no brute world, only an elaborated world": Merleau-Ponty on the interesubjecctive constitiuton of the world', *South African Journal of Philosophy*, 32:4, pp. 355–71.

Mordechai, G. (2011), 'Listening as embracing the other: Martin Buber's philosophy of dialogue', *Educational Theory*, 61:2, pp. 207–19.

Murray, A. (2010), *Agamben*, Abingdon: Routledge.

Nancy, J.-L. (1991), *The Inoperative Community* (trans. P. Connor, L. Garbus, M. Holland, and S. Sawhney), Minneapolis: University of Minnesota Press.

Nancy, J.-L. (1993), *The Birth to Presence* (trans. B. Holmes and others), Stanford: Stanford University Press.

Nancy, J.-L. (2000), *Being Singular Plural* (trans. R. D. Richardson and A. E. O'Byrne), Stanford: Stanford University Press.

Nietzsche, F. (1989), 'On truth and lies in a nonmoral sense', in *Nietzsche on Rhetoric and Language* (trans. S. L. Gilman, C. Blair and D. J. Parent), Oxford: Oxford University Press, pp. 246–57.

Noys, B. (1997), 'Communicative unreason: Bataille and Habermas', *Theory, Culture & Society*, 14:1, pp. 59–75.

Noys, B. (2000), *Bataille: A Critical Introduction*, London: Pluto Press.

Olivier, B. (2009), *Philosophy and Communication: Collected Essays*, Lausanne: Peter Lang Group AG.

Peters, D. J. (2001), *Speaking into the Air: A History of the Idea of Communication*, Chicago: University of Chicago Press.

Pfuetze, P. (1961), *Self, Society, Existence*, Greenwood Press.

Pieper, J. (2010), *Tradition: Concept and Claim*, South Bend: St. Augustine's Press.

Pinchevski, A. (2005), *By Way of Interruption: Levinas and the Ethics of Communication*, Pittsburgh: Duquensne University Press.

Rasor, P. (2000), 'Intersubjective communication and the self in Wieman and Habermas', *American Journal of Theology & Philosophy*, 21:3, pp. 269–87.

Reinach, A. (2012), *The Apriori Foundation of the Civil Law* (ed. J. F. Cosby), Frankfurt: Ontos Verlag.

Ricoeur, P. (1967), *Husserl: An Analysis of His Phenomenology* (trans. E. G. Ballard and L. E. Embree), Evanston: Northwestern University Press.

Risser, J. (2016), 'Locating shared life in the "thou"', in T. Szanto and D. Moran (eds), *The Phenomenology of Sociality*, London: Routledge, pp. 29–41.

Risser, J. (2019), 'Hearing the other: Communication as shared life', *Journal of Applied Hermeneutics*, Article 8, pp. 1–17.

Roffe, J. (2004), 'Ethics', in J. Reynolds and J. Roffe (eds), *Understanding Derrida*, London: Continuum, pp. 37–45.

Ross, M. (2013), *An Alternative Path: The Intellectual Legacy of James Carey*, Columbia: University of South Carolina.

Sanders, M. (2008), 'Intersubjectivity and alterity', in R. Diprose and J. Reynolds (eds), *Merleau-Ponty Key Concepts*, London: Routledge, pp. 142–51.

Scherto, G. (2015), 'Holding oneself open in a conversation: Gadamer's philosophical hermeneutics and the ethics of dialogue', *Journal of Dialogue Studies*, 3:1, pp. 9–28.

Schutz, A. (1950), 'Language, language disturbances, and the texture of consciousness', *Social Research*, 17:3, pp. 365–95.

Schutz, A. (1962), *Collected Papers I: The Problem of Social Reality*, The Hague: Martinus Nijhoff.

Schutz, A. (1967), *The Phenomenology of the Social World* (trans. G. Walsh), Evanston: Northwestern University Press.

Schutz, A. (1970), *Collected Papers III Studies in Phenomenolgical Philosophy*, The Hague: Martinus Nijhoff.

Schutz, A. (1976), *Collected Papers II Studies in Social Theory*, The Hague: Martinus Nijhoff.

Schutz, A. and Luckmann, T. (1974), *The Structures of the Lifeworld Vol. 1* (trans. R. M. Zaner and H. T. Engelhardt, Jr), London: Heinemann.

Schutz, A. and Luckmann, T. (1989), *The Structures of the Lifeworld Vol. 11* (trans. R. M. Zaner and D.J. Parent), London: Heinemann.

Scruton, R. (2017), *Conservatism: Ideas in Profile*, London: Profile Books.

Sella, Z. K. (2007), 'The journey of ritual communication', *Studies in Communication Sciences*, pp. 103–24.

Smith, T. (1931), 'The social philosophy of George Herbert Mead', *American Journal of Sociology*, 37:3, pp. 368–85.

Sokolowski, R. (2002), 'Semiotics in Husserl's logcal investigations', in D. Zahavi and F. Stjernfelt (eds), *One Hundred Years of Phenomenology*, Amsterdam: Kleweeer Academic Publishers, pp. 171–83.

Stalmaszczyk, P. and Oleksy, W. (2014), 'Philosophical and communicative turns in the study of language,' in W. Szubko-Sitarek, L. Salski, and P. Stalmaszczyk (eds), *Language Learning, Discourse and Communication*, Cham: Springer International Publishing, pp. 229–41.

Starwaska, B. (2009), *Between You and I: Dialogical Phenomenology*, Ohio University Press.

Subtil, F. (2014), 'James W Carey's cultural approach of communication', *Intercom – Revista Brasileira de Ciencias da Comunicaçǎo*, 37:1, pp. 19–24.

Taylor, C. (1991), *The Ethics of Authenticity*, Cambridge, MA: Harvard University Press.

Tejera, V. (1988), *Semiotics from Peirce to Barthes*, Koln: Brill.

ten Bos, R. (2005), 'Giorgio Agamben and the community without identity', *Sociological Review*, 53:1, p. 16–29

Tönnies, F. (2001), *Community and Civil Society* (trans. M. Hollis), Cambridge: Cambridge University Press.

Tremblay, T. (2016), 'Whatever singluarity, negative community and literature (perhaps)', *Countertext*, 2:1, pp. 44–54.

Trujillo, J. (2018), 'Intersubjectivity and the sociology of Alfred Schutz', *Bulletin d'Analyse Phénoménologique*, 14:7, pp. 1–30.

Vejera, V. (1986), 'Community, communication, and meaning: Theories of Buchler and Habermas', *Symbolic Interaction*, 9:1, pp. 83–104.

Vološinov, V. (1986), *Marxism and the Philosophy of Language* (trans. L. Matejka and I. R. Titunik), Cambridge, MA: Harvard University Press.

Watkin, W. (2014), *Agamben and Indifference*, London: Rowman and Littlefield International Ltd.

Womack, P. (2011), *Dialogue*, London: Routledge.

Ying Kwok, L. (2004), 'Intersubjectivity and phenomenology of the other: 135', in *Space Time and Culture* (eds David Carr and Cheung Chan-Fai), Dordrecht: Springer Science+Business Media, pp. 135–58.

Young, I. M. (1990), *Justice and the Politics of Difference*, Princeton: Princeton University Press.

Young, R. (1989), 'Not revolutionary: But communicating', *Oxford Literary Review*, pp. 213–25, https://www.euppublishing.com/doi/abs/10.3366/olr.1989.010?role=tab. Accessed 4 February 2025.

Zahavi, D. (2001), 'Beyond empathy: Phenomenological approaches to intersubjectivity', in *Between Ourselves: Second-Person Issues in the Study of Consciousness*, pp. 151–67.

Zaner, R. (1961), 'Theory of intersubjectivity: Alfred Schutz', *Social Research*, 28:1, pp. 71–93.

Index

G

H

I

J

K

L

www.ingramcontent.com/pod-product-compliance
Lightning Source LLC
LaVergne TN
LVHW080019131225
827248LV00003B/10